CW01020657

Rover and the Cows

Rover and the Cows

... And 30 Other Bible-Based Meditations

Series # 9

Roger Ellsworth

Unless otherwise noted, Scripture quotations are taken from the New King James Version®. Copyright © 1982 by Thomas Nelson. Used by permission. All rights reserved.

Copyright © 2018, Roger Ellsworth

All rights reserved. No part of this book may be reproduced, scanned, or distributed in any printed or electronic form without permission.

First Edition: 2018

ISBN: 978-0-9996559-7-9

201800829LSI

Great Writing Publications
www.greatwriting.org
Taylors, SC

www.greatwriting.org

Purpose

My Coffee Cup Meditations are short, easy-to-read, engagingly presented devotions based on the Bible, the Word of God. Each reading takes a single idea or theme and develops it in a thought-provoking way so that you are inspired to consider the greatness of God, the relevance of the good news of the life, death, resurrection, and coming-again of Jesus, and are better equipped for life in this world and well prepared for the world to come.

www.mycoffeecupmeditations.com

https://www.facebook.com/MyCoffeeCupMeditations/

Dedication

To

Wanda Rogers

Accomplished pianist and faithful friend

About This Book

This book is the result of the labors Roger Ellsworth and the thought he has given to various passages of Scripture over the years. You may read more about Roger on page 141.

We hope you will enjoy these Bible-based meditations. We would love to hear from you, so please send us a note to tell us what you think—which ones you liked most, and how they made a difference in your life or in the life of a family member, friend, or work associate. To reach us online, go to www.mycoffeecupmeditations.com/contact

MY COFFEE-CUP

MEDITATIONS

Table of Contents

The App

www.mycoffeecupmeditations.com

Be sure you get the app!

-1-

From God's Word, the Bible...

Whatever your hand finds to do, do it with your might; for there is
no work or device or knowledge or wisdom in the grave
where you are going.

Ecclesiastes 9:10

Rover and the Cows

We finally decided it would be best to let Rover retire. Rover was our dog through my childhood years. When he was just a pup, Dad trained him to "get the cows." That meant Rover was supposed to find the cows in the pasture and herd them to the barn.

I used to marvel at Rover. Milking time would come, and Dad would say: "Rover, get the cows!" But Rover wouldn't immediately dash off as one might expect. He would listen until he heard the bell that Dad had put around the neck of one of the cows. Then he would dash off, find the cows, and slowly herd them home. It was obvious that he relished doing his job. It was something that made him feel proud.

Rover did a good job for a long time. But as he began to age, his interest in getting the cows began to wane. It was no longer something that he wanted to do. It may have been the accumulating aches and pains of old age that caused him to hate the job that he used to love. But the change was evident for all to see. We would tell him to get the cows, and he would look away. He might even growl. When we insisted, he would finally and reluctantly go. The most obvious change was in the way he brought the cows home. Instead of slowly herding them, he began to drive them as fast as he could. When the cows got to the barn, they would be winded and sweaty.

So there was nothing to do except let Rover retire and drop his monthly social security check in the mail. Rover seemed to enjoy his retirement, most of which he spent sleeping in the warm sunshine and perhaps nostalgically recalling the glory days when he happily went to the get the cows.

Finally, the end came for Rover. I arrived home one day from my college commute to hear my Dad say: "I've got a job for you to do. I want you to bury Rover." It was one sad job. The tears flowed as I shoveled the dirt over my true and faithful friend.

As the years slide by and the aches and pains accumulate, I understand more and more Rover's desire to retire. Having retired from the pastorate a few years ago, I can say that retirement is more than okay. If I had known I was going to enjoy it so much, I would have done it long before I did! But there are dangers associated with it. We must never allow ourselves to think that we can retire from living for the glory of the Lord. We may find it necessary to step aside from "getting the cows," that is, from those ministries that call for the physical and mental strength of youth. But that doesn't mean we stop serving the Lord altogether. We older saints can strive to excel in prayer to the Lord and encouragement to others. I have benefited much from senior saints who have given themselves to these things. I now hope I can follow their good example.

The text above tells us to do with all our might whatever our "hand finds to do." My hand doesn't find as much to do as it did several years ago, but the things it does find to do are to be done heartily as unto the Lord.

When we find our interest in the work of the Lord faltering, we need to look to the Lord for more strength and motivation. Let our motto always be "looking unto Jesus" (Heb. 12:2). Looking to Him as He died in our stead on the cross will always increase our interest in the things of God and our strength for serving Him.

I've often been asked over the years if animals will be in heaven. I never hesitate to say that they will. The salvation of human beings is only one part of God's plan of redemption. The other part is God putting this physical order back to where it was before sin entered (Rom. 8:18-22). Since animals were part of the original creation, I expect them to be present in the new creation.

I hope my good friend Rover will be there. Perhaps there will even be occasion for me to say to him: "Come on Rover. Let's go get the cows."

-2-

From God's Word, the Bible...

And the Word became flesh and dwelt among us, and we beheld
His glory, the glory as of the only begotten of the Father,
full of grace and truth.

For He made Him who knew no sin to be sin for us, that we might
become the righteousness of God in Him.

For Christ also suffered once for sins, the just for the unjust, that
He might bring us to God, being put to death in the flesh
but made alive by the Spirit.

John 1:14; 2 Corinthians 5:21; 1 Peter 3:18

The Greatest of All Miracles

The Bible tells us about many miracles. Which is the greatest? I don't hesitate to say it's Jesus Himself.

The miracle of Jesus is threefold—His incarnation, His death, and His resurrection. The above texts set forth the threefold miracle of Jesus as Him being made flesh, made sin, and made alive.

First, there is *the miracle of Jesus' incarnation*, which C.S. Lewis calls "The Grand Miracle." He writes: "Every other miracle prepares for this, exhibits this, or results from this."

Think about it! The Second Person of the Trinity took our humanity without divesting Himself of His deity! So now we have the God-man—fully God and fully man!

The Apostle John saw proof of this as he was with Jesus for more than three years. During this time, he and the other disciples closely observed Jesus. They "beheld" Him.

There were times in which Jesus appeared to be nothing more than mere flesh, that is, as another human being! But every time John and the others thought they were seeing another man in Jesus, He would, as it were, pull back the robe of His humanity so they could see the underlying deity.

Then there is *the miracle of Jesus' death*. Some look at Jesus dying on the cross and say: "There surely is no miracle in a man dying! Nothing is more commonplace than that!"

We may very well be inclined to say that if we think of Jesus' death in physical terms only. But this wasn't just another man dying another death. It was much more than that. The Apostle Paul reveals the much more when he says Christ was "made sin" for us.

Yes, Jesus died physically in the most horrible way imaginable. But the real suffering was enduring the penalty for sin, which is eternal separation from God! While Jesus was on the cross, He actually suffered an eternity's worth of separation from God so all who believe in Him don't have to experience that same separation themselves. That's why Jesus cried: "My God, My God, why have You forsaken Me?" (Matt. 27:46).

How could Jesus in the space of the six hours He was on the cross experience an eternity's worthy of God's wrath? We've noticed that He was God in human flesh. As God, He was an infinite person, and as an infinite person He could receive in a finite length of time an infinite amount of wrath. Jesus, as an infinite person, could receive in a finite length of time what we as finite people would have to receive in an infinite amount of time.

The miracle of Jesus' death is that He bore the weight of all our sins.

The miracle of the incarnation led to the miracle of the cross, and the miracle of the cross led to *the miracle of Jesus' resurrection*.

It was essential that Jesus die the special kind of death upon which He and the Father had agreed. It was essential for Him to receive the penalty for those sinners who would believe on Him so that there would be no penalty left for them.

But as vital as the cross was, it would have been to no avail if Jesus' body had rotted away in the tomb. His resurrection was also vital. It proved Him to be God in human flesh, and, in doing so, proved that His death on the cross was of infinite value. It also proved that God was entirely satisfied with the death of Christ in the place of sinners. God is the One whom we have offended through our sins, and it is God who must be satisfied. The fact that God is the One who raised Jesus from the dead proves that God was satisfied with His redeeming death.

In one sense, the cross was the verdict of sinful men on Jesus. By nailing Him there, they were pronouncing Him to be a fraud. The resurrection was the verdict of God on Jesus, and what a radically different verdict it was! God was reversing or setting aside the verdict of sinful men on His Son, and pronouncing His own verdict on Him. By raising Jesus from the dead, God was setting the record straight regarding His Son.

The incarnation, death, and resurrection join their voices to point us to the miracle of Jesus. Have you heeded their voices?

-3-

From God's Word, the Bible...

And we know that all things work together for good to those who
love God, to those who are the called according to His purpose.

Romans 8:28

Father, Whate'er of Earthly Bliss

An old Welsh hymn uses the memorable phrase "life's cruel pounding." I would say Anne Steele could easily relate to that phrase. One blow came when her mother died when Anne was only three. Another blow came when at age nineteen she suffered a serious injury to her hip after being thrown from a horse. Yet another blow came when her fiancée drowned the day before their wedding. Further difficulties came her way when her stepmother and her sister died. Added to these were the burdens of caring for her sick father for many years as well as her own ongoing health problems.

In the midst of it all, Anne found comfort in writing hymns and poems (well over three hundred in number).

When her fiancé died, Anne took up her pen to write a long poem entitled *When I Survey Life's Varied Scene*. The last three verses of that poem made their way into many hymnals under the title *Father, Whate'er of Earthly Bliss*.

These three verses (and the long poem from which they

were taken) are a prayer. Isn't it interesting that Anne chose to let the pounding of life drive her to God instead of away from Him? Life pounded, and she prayed! Prayer is always a strong and sure refuge in our hours of great need. We're bound to regret not availing ourselves of that refuge more often. Many have looked back over their lives with the wish that they would have prayed more. I've never heard of anyone wishing that he or she had prayed less.

Anne's prayer is bulging with trust. She says:

> *Father, whate'er of earthly bliss,*
> *Thy sovereign will denies;*
> *Accepted at Thy throne of grace,*
> *Let this petition rise:*

Yes, life had severely wounded her, but she rested in the knowledge that the sovereign God of the universe was her Father, and His throne was one of grace. The fact God is sovereign means that He rules the lives of His people to the glory of His name. Nothing comes our way apart from His knowledge and purpose. Nothing that happens to us gets around God. Everything springs from His heart and passes through His hands.

Our flesh screams out in protest: "You mean this hardship has come from God? Why would He do such a thing?"

We want answers, and we want them now! But we must wait for our answers, and we must believe as we wait that, when the answers come, they will reveal God's loving heart. When the book of explanation is finally read, we will not see any flaws in God's governance but only in our faith.

With confidence that God's throne is one of grace, Anne offered some petitions to the Lord. Verses two and three of her hymn relate them:

Give me a calm, thankful heart,
From every murmur free;
The blessings of Thy grace impart,
And let me live to Thee.

Let the sweet hope that Thou art mine,
My path of life attend;
Thy presence through my journey shine,
And bless its happy end.

In the midst of her trials, she wanted to have "a calm, thankful heart" and to be free from "every murmur." She didn't want to go through life complaining about what the Lord had sent her way. She understood that whether life be happy or sad, the Christian's business is always the same, that is, to live for the Lord.

Anne didn't ask for an easier life. She had the calm assurance that she belonged to the Lord. This was the "sweet hope" that she wanted to "attend" her as she walked the "path of life." She wanted the Lord to make His presence known to her as she journeyed along, and she wanted to know His blessing as she reached life's happy end. Life itself may be difficult for the Christian, but the ending is happy because it sweeps us into that realm where we will see our Lord and know difficulties no more.

By the way, Anne did indeed have a "happy end." When she died at age sixty-two in 1778, she was very peaceful. And her last words were: "I know that my Redeemer liveth."

How thankful we should be for that word "Redeemer"! It refers, of course, to the Lord Jesus Christ. He came from heaven to bring us back from sin and to God. Knowing Christ as our Redeemer outweighs the heaviest hardship, or, for that matter, all of our hardships.

-4-

From God's Word, the Bible...

But the righteousness of faith speaks in this way, "Do not say in your heart, 'Who will ascend into heaven?'" (that is, to bring Christ down from above) or, "'Who will descend into the abyss?'" (that is, to bring Christ up from the dead).

Romans 10:6-7

What's Your Strategy?

Many these days admit that the United States is more divided than at any time since the Civil War. At the mere mention of any issue, conservatives take one side and liberals the other.

There is still one issue on which we must all agree. We are going to die (Heb. 9:27). Yes, Christians who are living when Jesus comes will be exempt from death (1 Thess. 5:16-17), but the vast majority of us will die.

So here's my question: What's your strategy for facing the sobering reality of death?

Many will deny it, but most of us intuitively know that death is not the end. It isn't the cessation of existence. God has put eternity into our hearts (Eccl. 3:11).

So in asking for your strategy for facing death, I'm asking for your strategy for entering eternity. A strategy is a plan of action that is designed to achieve a desirable end. Do you have a plan of action for dying and going into eternity? What we really need is for someone who is an expert on such matters to come and help us. If we could only reach up to heaven and bring someone down! He could explain these things to us! And we would be very happy to hear and to heed!

If we could only find someone who has actually conquered death, someone who arose from the grave! He could give us the strategy we need for facing death! We would be more than ready to listen if such a person could be found!

The Bible tells us to stop our search for someone to come down from heaven or to come up from the grave. It's not that such a person can't be found. It's rather that such a person has been found. There's no need to search further. The need now is for people to listen to Him.

This person is Jesus Christ. He is the One who came down from heaven. Here's what He said to Nicodemus: "No one has ascended to heaven but He who came down from heaven, that is, the Son of Man. . . ." (John 3:13).

Jesus is also the One who came up from the grave. Here are His words about that: "I am He who lives, and was dead, and behold, I am alive forevermore. Amen. And I have the keys of Hades and of Death" (Rev. 1:18).

Jesus is the One, and the only One, who can speak with authority about dying and going to heaven. He came from heaven, He died, and He rose again.

How can we be sure that Jesus came from heaven? He did things that could only be done by someone from heaven. Benjamin Warfield explained His miracles in this way:

When our Lord came down to earth He drew heaven with Him. The signs which accompanied His ministry were but the trailing clouds of glory which He brought from heaven which is His home.[1]

---

[1] Benjamin B. Warfield, *Counterfeit Miracles* (Edinburgh: The Banner of Truth Trust, 1972), p.3.

And how can we be sure that Jesus arose from the grave? The Apostle Paul gives us the answer in these words: ". . . this thing was not done in a corner" (Acts 26:26).

Jesus' resurrection wasn't hidden away from public view. Many saw the empty tomb and the risen Christ.

But there's a problem. Multitudes who think they would be willing to listen to such a person aren't willing to listen to Christ at all. It's just like Jesus said to Nicodemus: "Most assuredly, I say to you, We speak what We know and testify what We have seen, and you do not receive Our witness" (John 3:11).

Jesus came from heaven to speak to us about heaven, but we must be willing to receive His words. He came from heaven to receive on the cross the penalty for sinners so those sinners may go to heaven. But we must be willing to repent of our sins and trust in Him in His saving work on the cross.

Jesus arose from the grave to prove that He was indeed from heaven and that what He did on the cross is sufficient for our sins. And now Paul says to us: ". . . if you confess with your mouth the Lord Jesus and believe in your heart that God has raised Him from the dead, you will be saved" (Rom. 10:9).

Jesus is the strategy we all need for facing death and going to heaven. Have you made Him your strategy?

-5-

From God's Word, the Bible...

"Go and tell Hananiah, saying, 'Thus says the LORD: "You have broken the yokes of wood, but you have made in their place yokes of iron."

Jeremiah 28:13

Yokes of Wood and Iron

A yoke was a wooden device placed over the neck of an ox to enable it to pull a wagon or a plow. Sometimes oxen were "yoked" together as a team. The yoke represented servitude.

As he declared the word of the Lord to the people of Judah, Jeremiah also wore a yoke. No joke—this prophet wore a yoke!

Jeremiah's yoke was intended to convey this solemn truth: God had put Babylon's yoke of servitude on Judah (Jer. 27:2,11). The Babylonians had already taken some of Judah's citizens into captivity, and another invasion would soon come. Resistance from the people of Judah would only lead to greater disaster (27:8,11). The need, then, was for the Jewish people to submit to the yoke of Babylon as an ox submits to the yoke of its master.

We must not think Jeremiah's message consisted only of gloom and doom. He also stressed the grace of God, which would produce the release of the Jews from Babylon after seventy years.

Even with this note of grace, Jeremiah's message wasn't a popular one. A lot of people didn't like it. Hananiah was one of them. Believing that God had already broken the yoke of Babylon and that those who had been taken captive would soon return (vv. 2-4), Hananiah decided to take bold action. He confronted Jeremiah at the temple in the presence of the priests and other worshipers, took the yoke from his neck, and smashed it (v. 10). He then declared: "Thus says the LORD: 'Even so I will break the yoke of Nebuchadnezzar king of Babylon from the neck of all nations within the space of two full years'" (v. 11).

Wonderful, but wrong! That was Hananiah's message.

After this incident, the Lord told Jeremiah to go to Hananiah with this message: "Thus says the LORD: 'You have broken the yokes of wood, but you have made in their place yokes of iron'" (v. 13).

The forthcoming captivity to the Babylonians was a yoke of iron. It couldn't be broken. It would definitely happen (v. 14).

But there was more. A yoke of iron is heavier than one of wood. By his false message, Hananiah had made things worse. He had caused the people to "trust in a lie" (v. 15). The captivity would be hard for those who knew it was coming. It would be even harder for those who believed it wasn't coming.

It was the Lord who was bringing captivity to the people of Judah. In telling them that it wouldn't happen, Hananiah was preaching "rebellion against the LORD" (v. 16). Part of the price for his false message was his own death, which came within two months of his encounter with Jeremiah (vv.1, 17).

That long-ago day may seem to have no value in this day when most people know little or nothing about prophets,

Babylonians or yokes. But the truth is that old day is this day. Hananiah and Jeremiah are still with us. Hananiah wants to make people feel good. He doesn't want them to be weighed down with talk about sin and judgment, and the need for repentance.

But then there is Jeremiah. He talks about those very things that Hananiah spurns. He talks about the reality of our sins, and he tells us about judgment to come. He calls us to repent of our sins, and he assures us that God will graciously forgive us if we do repent.

Hananiah's message sounds good and makes us feel good, but it is Jeremiah's message that will actually do us good.

The passing of time proved Jeremiah's message to be correct. The Babylonians did come once again to Judah and took most of the people into captivity, and after seventy years the Jews were released from their captivity and restored to their homeland.

Hananiah's smashing of Jeremiah's yoke makes me think of another object of wood—the cross of Christ. As Hananiah hated Jeremiah's yoke, so there are modern Hananiahs who hate that cross of wood. They want to smash that cross, that is, destroy its message. They are "enemies of the cross of Christ" (Phil. 3:18).

Those who hate the message of the cross can never destroy it. The cross lives on! In hating that cross they only succeed in making for themselves a yoke of iron—a much heavier burden—the burden of eternal separation from God.

-6-

From God's Word, the Bible...

You therefore must endure hardship as
a good soldier of Jesus Christ.

2 Timothy 2:3

A Soldier of the Cross

Isaac Watts didn't look much like a soldier. He was stumpy and homely. Stumpy? Yes, he was five feet tall. Homely? Yes, that too. He had a large head, small eyes, and a hooked nose. Some of his unappealing appearance may have resulted from a serious bout with smallpox when he was very young. Whatever the cause, it proved to be very costly to him. A beautiful young woman declined his proposal of marriage with these words: "Mr. Watts, I only wish I could say that I admire the casket as much as I admire the jewel."

We understand that the term "casket" in those days often referred to a jewel box. As a person, Watts was a jewel, but, alas, his body made a very poor jewel box.

When he was very young, Watts began to write poetry. And it wasn't long until he began to notice the singing in his church. After a service in which it was notably poor, Watts said to his father: "The singing of God's praise is the part of worship nearest heaven and its performance among us is the worst on earth."

His father responded by urging him to do something

about the situation. Young Isaac did exactly that. He spent that afternoon writing the hymn *Behold the Glories of the Lamb*, which his church sang that very night. They loved it and urged him to write more. Write he did, producing 750 hymns and earning for himself the title "The Father of English Hymnody." Some of his best-known hymns are *When I Survey the Wondrous Cross*; *At the Cross; Jesus Shall Reign*; *O God, Our Help in Ages Past,* and *Joy to the World*.

Watts was also a pastor. In 1701 at age twenty-six, he became the pastor of the Mark Lane Independent Church in London. Although often plagued by ill health, he continued to serve there until his death on November 25, 1748.

So Watts' life often brought him hardship and disappointment, but nothing deterred him from serving the Lord. Those who use the slightest inconvenience as an excuse to step aside from service would do well to learn from him. In the hymn *Am I a Soldier of the Cross?* Watts asks:

> *Must I be carried to the skies*
> *On flowery beds of ease. . . ?*

Watts answered that question for himself with an emphatic "No!" He didn't think his difficulties entitled him to "flowery beds of ease." He was a soldier of the cross.

The author of Hebrews urged his readers to be "looking unto Jesus" (Heb. 12:2). We should do so every day and in every way. When we look to Him on this matter of difficulties, what do we see? The first thing is this: no one ever had to endure more hardship than He. The next thing is this: Jesus didn't let the adversities He encountered drive Him away from the work that He came to this earth to perform—the glorious work of redemption. If He had done so, there would have been no salvation from sin and no eternal life for any of us.

We may have allowed ourselves to think from time to time that the work of redemption was, as the saying goes, "a piece of cake" for Jesus. After all, He was God! How hard could it have been for Him? We won't have the complete answer to that question until we finally get to heaven. When we get that answer, we will be astounded. We do know that His saving work:

- caused Him to cross the incredible chasm between being the Prince of heaven and being a helpless baby in a manger;
- caused Him to leave the courts of heaven where the triune God was perfectly loved, worshiped, and obeyed, and come into this realm in which there was much of sin and little of love, worship, and obedience toward God. How it must have grieved Him to live every day with sin and shame all around!
- caused Him to go to the cross where He actually endured the wrath of God in the place of unworthy, undeserving sinners.

When we feel as if our problems exempt us from serving the Lord, we do well to recall Isaac Watts, who didn't opt out from serving God. We do even better to think of Jesus: "For consider Him who endured such hostility from sinners against Himself, lest you become weary and discouraged in your souls" (Heb. 12:3).

-7-

From God's Word, the Bible...

But God forbid that I should boast except in the cross of our Lord
Jesus Christ, by whom the world has been crucified to me,
and I to the world.

Galatians 6:14

Surveying the Cross

Isaac Watts, a soldier of the cross, wrote some marvelous hymns about the Lord Jesus dying on the cross. Two of my favorites are *When I Survey the Wondrous Cross* and *At the Cross* (or *Alas, and Did My Savior Bleed*?).

In the first of these he calls us to "survey" the cross. To "survey" something is to do far more than casually glance at it. It is to thoroughly inspect something until we can form a proper appraisal of it. How many of us can say that we have surveyed the cross of Christ? How many of us have formed a true and accurate appraisal of it?

Watts wants us to look steadily at the cross until we see the "wondrous" nature of it. A wondrous thing is something that causes us to marvel with amazement. Part of the sadness of this age is that we marvel at things that aren't really all that marvelous and we fail to marvel at those things that are.

The marvel of the cross lies in the One who was there and in what He was doing there.

Who was on that cross? Watts tells us it was "the Prince of glory." It was the One who came from the glories of heaven to this earth. It was the glorious Son of God who left behind all the glorious trappings of heaven and the praises of the angels so that He could take our humanity. No, He didn't lay aside His deity to do this. God can't quit being God. It's rather that He added to His deity our humanity.

The person who was on that cross is part of what makes it wondrous. The other part of what makes it wondrous is what He was doing there. Watts makes this explicit in *At the Cross*:

> *Was it for crimes that I have done,*
> *He groaned upon the tree?*

Jesus was not on the cross for Himself. He was not there because He deserved to be. He was there because we deserve to be. It was our "crimes" that put Him there. Our crimes are our sins. Sins are crimes. Our sins are lawbreaking. God has given us laws by which we are to live, and we choose to break them rather than keep them.

The Lord Jesus was on the cross as if He were a lawbreaker even though He Himself had never broken any of God's laws. He was there to receive the penalty for our lawbreaking.

Isn't the penalty for our sins far greater than physical death? Yes! Now we're getting to the very heart of the cross. It was far more than Jesus dying physically. How many of us have surveyed the cross enough to realize this? It was Jesus receiving the wrath of God on our lawbreaking. It was Jesus enduring an eternity's worth of separation from God so that all who repent of their sins and trust in Him don't have to endure that same penalty.

The Prince of Glory on the cross to receive my hell—that's the wonder of the cross! Watts saw it and marveled. Have we seen it?

Once we see what Watts saw, we can easily understand these words from *When I Survey*:

Forbid it, Lord, that I should boast,
Save in the death of Christ my God!
All the vain things that charm me most,
I sacrifice them to His blood.

Were the whole realm of nature mine,
That were a present far too small;
Love so amazing, so divine,
Demands my life, my soul, my all.

This is the response of adoring praise and firm resolve. Has the Prince of Glory received the wrath of God for me? I will give up "the vain things" of this world to live for Him. I will give Him "my life, my soul, my all."

We find a similar response in *At the Cross*:

But drops of grief can ne'er repay
The debt of love I owe:
Here, Lord, I give myself away,
'Tis all that I can do!

Our choice is never between a cross-centered Christianity and another kind of Christianity for this simple reason: there is no Christianity apart from the cross. The choice is rather this: Will we intently study the cross until we see the wonder of it, or will we only lightly ponder it?

-8-

From God's Word, the Bible...

So the ransomed of the LORD shall return,
And come to Zion with singing,
With everlasting joy on their heads.
They shall obtain joy and gladness;
Sorrow and sighing shall flee away.

Isaiah 51:11

We're Marching
to Zion

The year 1707 saw the release of Isaac Watts' stirring, happy hymn, *We're Marching to Zion*. I well remember the small church in which I grew up triumphantly singing these words (the refrain was added later by Robert Lowry):

Come, we that love the Lord,
And let our joys be known;
Join in a song with sweet accord,
And thus surround the throne.
We're marching to Zion, Beautiful, beautiful Zion;
We're marching upward to Zion, The beautiful city of God.

The word "Zion" sometimes appears in Scripture as a reference to the city of Jerusalem. In other places, it refers to the heavenly city, the New Jerusalem, which is the destiny of all of God's people. It's the heavenly Zion that Watts' hymn puts before us. The message of the hymn is quite plain. The thought of going to heaven ought to so fill our hearts with joy that we can't help but sing.

Watts took a dim view of those who claim to have their sins forgiven and to be on their way to heaven but refuse to sing:

> *Let those refuse to sing,*
> *Who never knew our God;*
> *But children of the heav'nly King,*
> *May speak their joys abroad.*

Someone might excuse himself for not singing by saying: "I will wait until I get to heaven." Watts' response to such thinking is found here:

> *The men of grace have found*
> *Glory begun below;*
> *Celestial fruits on earthly ground*
> *From faith and hope may grow.*

> *The hill of Zion yields*
> *A thousand sacred sweets,*
> *Before we reach the heav'nly fields,*
> *Or walk the golden streets.*

Heaven is the future possession of God's people, but it's also our present possession. Glory has already begun here "below." "Celestial fruits" can grow here on "earthly ground" as God's people exercise "faith and hope." Faith is the confidence, the calm assurance, of what we as Christians possess through Christ. Hope is stronger. It is eagerly looking forward to possessing that which we are sure of. Faith makes us sure. Hope makes us eager.

Watts also affirms that heaven is even now yielding for

us "a thousand sacred sweets." These are to be enjoyed now before we reach "the heavenly fields or walk the golden streets."

What are these "sweets"? They are the blessings—the spiritual privileges—that are ours to enjoy as we journey to our heavenly home. These may not be exactly one thousand in number, but they are numerous—far more than most of us realize. When we get to heaven and look back over our earthly pilgrimage, we will be amazed at the number of ways God blessed us.

This is a world of tears, but all our tears aren't enough to destroy the joy of knowing that heaven will be our home. So Watts urges us to put things in their proper perspective:

> *Then let our songs abound,*
> *And every tear be dry:*
> *We're marching through Immanuel's ground*
> *To fairer worlds on high.*

The Bible doesn't tell us to never cry. It rather tells us to use our hope of heaven to dry our tears.

In pointing us to heaven and urging us to rejoice in it, Watts doesn't fail to remind us of the way to get there. We walk to heaven on "Immanuel's ground."

The name "Immanuel" means "God with us" (Matt. 1:23), and it refers to the Lord Jesus who left the glories of heaven to come to this earth in our humanity. He came in flesh to be with us (John 1:14), but He also came to do something for us, that is, to die on the cross so that we might be saved.

There has to be ground on which we walk if we are to journey to heaven, and we walk on it by repenting of our sins and trusting in Him.

-9-

From God's Word, the Bible...

Then Ebed-Melech the Ethiopian said to Jeremiah, "Please put these old clothes and rags under your armpits, under the ropes." And Jeremiah did so.

Jeremiah 38:12

Rags and Old Clothes Never Looked So Good

One of the many joys of heaven will be meeting people of faith who appear only briefly in the Bible. I'm referring to people who emerged from obscurity to boldly act for the Lord before going into obscurity again. One of these is Ebed-Melech, the man of rags and old clothes.

We must, however, start with the prophet Jeremiah. He was God's truth-teller in a truth-hating time. The truth Jeremiah told the people of Judah was quite simple. Because of their continued disobedience to God and their refusal to repent, God was bringing calamity upon them in the form of the Babylonian Empire (Jer. 38:1-3).

Lots of people hated that message, and they hated Jeremiah for preaching it. The Jeremiah-haters thought his message must be false because it was unpleasant and made them uncomfortable. Multitudes hold the same view in our era!

Four men—Shephatiah, Gedaliah, Jucal, and Pashhur—decided to take action. They went to their king, the lily-livered Zedekiah, and asked permission to do away with the prophet. The king lamely responded to their request with these reprehensible words: "Look, he is in your hand. For the king can do nothing against you" (v. 5).

So these men, in one of the foulest of all deeds, seized Jeremiah and lowered him into the mud of a waterless cistern (v. 6). They wanted him dead, but they didn't want to actually shed his blood. So they would let him die from having no food or water and being in the cold and the damp. Heartless men, these four!

That brings us to Ebed-Melech, an Ethiopian eunuch who served in the king's palace. He could have excused himself from taking any action by telling himself that it was none of his business or that any action he took would only bring him trouble. If such thoughts entered his mind, he quickly dismissed them. He went boldly to the king who was sitting in a public place and spoke about Jeremiah in the cistern (vv. 7-9). Now the king was on the spot. While Jeremiah wasn't popular, few of Judah's citizens would have approved of him being tortured.

The king told Ebed-Melech to take thirty men with him to get Jeremiah out of the cistern. Why take thirty men? The king may have thought that Ebed-Melech would need them to protect him as he raised Jeremiah from the cistern. Those who put Jeremiah in the cistern would surely have been happy for Ebed-Melech to join him there.

Thoughtful man that he was, Ebed-Melech took some "old clothes and old rags" (v.12) for Jeremiah to have some cushioning. Lifting him from the mire of that cistern would require no small amount of tugging!

Because Ebed-Melech so kindly delivered the prophet from the cistern, the Lord promised to deliver him from the

Babylonians (39:15-18).

How are we to explain Ebed-Melech? We surely have to trace his action back to God. We have to say that God's grace had so worked in his heart that he felt compassion for the prophet. We should learn from Ebed-Melech to show tender regard for those whom God has called to preach His Word (Matt. 10:41).

I see in Jeremiah's plight a picture of my own. As he was mired in the mud of that cistern, so I was once mired in the pit of sin and condemnation. And I see in Ebed-Melech a picture of the Lord Jesus Christ with a large difference. While Ebed-Melech used ropes, old clothes, and rags to raise Jeremiah from the cistern, the Lord Jesus Christ actually came into my cistern. He, who knew no sin, was made sin for me on the cross so that I could be delivered from it (2 Cor. 5:21).

Because of the saving grace of the Lord Jesus, I can now take as my own the words of David:

> *He also brought me up out of a horrible pit,*
> *Out of the miry clay,*
> *And set my feet upon a rock,*
> *And established my steps.*
> *He has put a new song in my mouth –*
> *Praise to our God. . .*
> (Ps. 40:2-3a)

When I meet Ebed-Melech in heaven's glory, I will want to hear his account of pulling Jeremiah from the cistern. But I won't be surprised if he says: "Let me tell you, instead, about my cistern of sin that was far deeper than Jeremiah's and of the Savior who is far greater than I."

-10-

From God's Word, the Bible...

O Zion,
You who bring good tidings,
Get up into the high mountain;
O Jerusalem,
You who bring good tidings,
Lift up your voice with strength,
Lift it up, be not afraid;
Say to the cities of Judah, "Behold your God!"

Isaiah 40:9

"Behold Your God"

We often find the word "behold" in Scripture. It's a strong word. It calls us not to merely look at something, but to actually see it. How often we look without really seeing! We can go further. The word "behold" calls us to look intently at something until we feel a sense of wonder and admiration.

The church of the Lord Jesus Christ needs to recover the art of beholding. She often seems to be like a factory with machines droning and people moving about with dull familiarity. We seem to think Christianity is a product that has to be properly packaged and marketed if we are to get people to "buy" it. More specifically, Christianity is often presented as a product that insures success and happiness in this life. If certain levers are pulled and certain buttons pushed, the product will be purchased, and the customer will be happy. So the factory drones on.

The Christian faith ought to thrill our souls. But there's little thrill in five principles for this, six keys to that, or four secrets for the other.

The prophet Isaiah was enabled by the Spirit of God to look into the future. He saw a sobering thing. Most of his people, the people of Judah, would be in captivity in faraway Babylon. Life there would become humdrum and monotonous without anything to inspire or thrill.

So prompted by the Spirit, Isaiah wrote words that would bring comfort and wonder to those poor captives. While they were there in Babylon, they would be inclined to see nothing but Babylonians, difficulties, and sorrows. The need would be for them to lift up their eyes to see something greater than their situation.

Isaiah was the man God had selected to be the bearer of good news to Zion and Jerusalem (each a name for the people of God) in their captivity. What was Isaiah to say to them? The first thing was this: "Behold your God!"

The prophet was calling those captives to think about their God until their hearts were saturated with His glory and wonder. God couldn't be seen with physical eyes, but He could be seen with the eyes of faith.

With that initial "behold" in place, Isaiah quickly added two more. They were to behold the Lord God coming "with a strong hand" to "reward" them and to care for them as a shepherd (vv. 10-11). And they were to behold Him as the One who counts all the nations, including Babylon, as "a drop in a bucket" (v. 15). The promise was that their great God would, in due time, deliver them from Babylon and bring them back to their homeland. What a deliverance that would be! But it was at best only a faint picture of a far greater deliverance, namely, that of sinful people through the redeeming work of Christ.

Each "behold" caused Isaiah to launch into a breathtaking description of the greatness of God.

One of our newer songs, *Behold Our God*, marvelously gathers up Isaiah's description of God in these words:

Who has held the oceans in His hands?
Who has numbered every grain of sand?
Kings and nations tremble at His voice
All creation rises to rejoice.

Who has given counsel to the Lord?
Who can question any of His words?
Who can teach the One Who knows all things?
Who can fathom all His wondrous deeds?

Who has felt the nails upon His hands
Bearing all the guilt of sinful man?
God eternal humbled to the grave
Jesus, Savior, risen now to reign!

Chorus:
Behold our God seated on His throne
Come, let us adore Him!
Behold our King! Nothing can compare,
Come, let us adore Him![2]

The reach of this song is truly thrilling, dropping, as it does, from the throne of the One who hold oceans and numbers grains of sand to the cross of Calvary where the Lord "felt the nails upon His hands" as He bore "the guilt of sinful man."

From his distant day, Isaiah calls to the church today. He calls us to stop focusing on the mundane and trivial and to behold our God, never forgetting as we do that the most glorious sight of Him is in His Son on the cross.

---

[2] *Behold Our God*, sovereigngracemusic.org/music/songs/behold-our-god-who-has-held-the-oceans/ Words and music by Ryan Baird, Jonathan Baird, Meghan Baird, and Stephen Altrogge. © 2011

-11-

From God's Word, the Bible...

The next day John saw Jesus coming toward him, and said,
"Behold! The Lamb of God who takes away the sin of the world!"

John 1:29

"Behold! the Lamb of God"

Any sensible list of the most astounding words ever spoken would have to include those of this verse. When John the Baptist saw Jesus approaching, he cried out: "Behold! The Lamb of God who takes away the sin of the world!"

John's was a Jewish audience. Those who heard this cry needed no explanation. Knowing what the lamb symbolized, they immediately knew what John the Baptist was saying about Jesus, and, yes, it was truly astounding.

Every year the Jews celebrated the Passover. That celebration commemorated the event of the release of their forefathers from slavery in Egypt many centuries in the past. How did that release come about? God sent His death angel over the land of Egypt to slay "the firstborn of man and the firstborn of animal" (Ex. 13:15). But He made a special provision for the Jews. They were to slay lambs and place their blood at the tops and at the sides of their doors. God promised that His angel would "pass over" every house marked with that blood (Ex. 12:3-7,13).

And those who heard John the Baptist's cry were also very familiar with Isaiah 53. A prophecy of the Messiah, it includes these words:

He was led as a lamb to the slaughter. . . (v. 7).

So John the Baptist was affirming in a powerful and un-mistakable way that Jesus was the long-awaited Messiah. That was astounding.

Sadly enough, many of those who heard John's announce-ment on that day had lost their grip on the work of their Messiah. Even though a dying Messiah was definitely in their Scriptures, many were looking for a political leader.

But Jesus came to be what the Old Testament pictured and prophesied. He came to be the Lamb of God, which is to say He came to be God's way to forgive sinners of their sins, so they wouldn't have to experience the condemnation that those sins deserve. And that way—let us be forever clear on this—was by Jesus being the substitute for those sinners. The slain lambs in the first Passover were essentially substitutes. Their blood was shed so the blood of the Jews' firstborn wouldn't have to be shed. To say Jesus is God's Lamb is to say that He, Jesus, was set forth by God to be the substitute for sinners. When He died on the cross, He received the wrath of God in the place of all who will trust in Him.

God's justice demands that the penalty for sin be paid. There's no way around that. But God's justice only demands that the penalty for sin be paid once, not twice. It would be unjust for God to demand payment twice. Here is the glory of the gospel—since Jesus made the payment for sinners on the cross, those who trust in Him don't have to make the payment again. They can rather sing with Elvina Hall:

Jesus paid it all,
All to Him I owe;
Sin had left a crimson stain,
He washed it white as snow.

And they can triumphantly and joyously take as their own these words from the Apostle Paul: "There is therefore now no condemnation to those who are in Christ Jesus. . ." (Rom. 8:1). And how do we get into Christ? We do so by renouncing every other hope for salvation and trusting wholly in His substitutionary work on the cross.

The Bible calls to us now to behold the Lamb, to look with wonder and amazement at Him dying on that cross. It calls us to marvel that on the cross Jesus received the wrath that we deserve.

We can only do this beholding now with the eyes of faith. But an indescribably glorious day is coming in which we will see Jesus, our Lamb, face to face. On that day, we will join in this glad anthem:

Worthy is the Lamb who was slain
To receive power and riches and wisdom,
And strength and honor and glory and blessing!
(Rev. 5:13)

Let's rejoice in Jesus, the wrath-bearing Lamb of God, but let's also remember that those who don't receive Him will one day cry to be hidden "from the wrath of the Lamb" (Rev. 6:16).

-12-

From God's Word, the Bible...

"Rejoice greatly, O daughter of Zion!
Shout, O daughter of Jerusalem!
Behold, your King is coming to you;
He is just and having salvation,
Lowly and riding on a donkey,
A colt, the foal of a donkey."

"Tell the daughter of Zion,
'Behold, your King is coming to you,
Lowly, and sitting on a donkey,
A colt, the foal of a donkey.'"

Zechariah 9:9; Matthew 21:5

"Behold, Your King"

It is the Passover season, and Jerusalem, filled with pilgrims, is abuzz. The buzz is about Jesus. Much of it is due to Him having raised Lazarus from the dead a few days back. That occurred in nearby Bethany.

On this particular Sunday, the Lord Jesus is in Bethany. Many people are there to watch His every move. Things begin to unfold quickly. Jesus gives two of His disciples kinglike commands about securing a donkey for Him to ride into Jerusalem. Some of the observers in Bethany begin to piece things together. Jesus is finally going to make His move. He is going to declare Himself to be the King of Israel. They run to Jerusalem to announce the news. Many there pour out of the city toward Bethany. Meanwhile, a large number is accompanying Jesus from Bethany. Somewhere between Bethany and Jerusalem the two crowds merge. Euphoria reigns as people spread their outer garments on the road along with palm branches that they had cut down. They suddenly join their voices in loudly crying:

"Hosanna to the Son of David!
'Blessed is He who comes
In the name of the Lord!'
Hosanna in the highest!"

None of this happens by accident. It is all a fulfillment of Zechariah's prophecy:

"Tell the daughter of Zion,
'Behold, your King is coming to you,
Lowly, and sitting on a donkey,
A colt, the foal of a donkey.'"

People welcoming their king! That's what we have here. It seems to be a wonderful thing. But something isn't right. Jesus is weeping as He approaches the city of Jerusalem (Luke 19:41-44).

What's wrong? While the people are beholding Jesus as their king and acclaiming Him as their king, they are in the grip of grievous error. They are beholding Jesus as the king they want Him to be instead of as the king He actually came to be. They are hailing Him as a mere temporal king, one who will free their nation from bondage to the Romans and usher in a golden age.

It's all right there in that word "Hosanna," which means "save now." They want a king who will save them politically, and will do it right now. But that's not the kind of king Jesus came to be.

And when they learn that Jesus isn't going to be the kind of king they want, they turn on Him. In one of the greatest ironies in all of history, many of those who are crying "Hosanna" on this Sunday will cry "Crucify" later that same week.

The Bible urges us to behold Jesus as our king, but it also

warns us to not repeat the error of those who swarm around Jesus as He enters Jerusalem. We are to behold Jesus as the king that He is, and not as the king that we want.

It's very easy for us to forget the words that Jesus would speak to Pilate later in this week: "My kingdom is not of this world" (John 18:36).

So the question before us is this: Are we properly beholding Jesus as our king? We can ask it in this way: Are we standing in awe before Jesus as the king that He came to be?

What kind of king did Jesus come to be? The multitude was correct to think of Jesus as a king bringing salvation. But they were wrong in their understanding of that salvation. It wasn't salvation from the Romans that Jesus was offering. It was rather salvation from another kind of bondage—one that was far worse—the bondage to sin and Satan.

This is the bondage Jesus came to break, and He broke it on the cross for all who will repent of their sins and trust in Him.

Jesus, our bondage-breaker, now rules in the hearts of all His people. And He rules over the bewildering events and circumstances of this world for the good of His people and the glory of His name. The day is coming in which the kingship of Jesus will be apparent to all. On that day, He will be universally acknowledged as King of kings and Lord of lords (Rev. 19:16). The choice before us is to either gladly bow before His kingship now in wondering admiration or to bow before it later when He comes to judge those who spurn His salvation.

-13-

From God's Word, the Bible...

Then Jesus came out, wearing the crown of thorns and the purple robe. And Pilate said to them, "Behold the Man!"

John 19:5

"Behold, the Man!"

Pontius Pilate, the Roman procurator of Judea, was a man with a dilemma on his hands. He knew that the religious leaders of the Jews wanted Jesus to be crucified. To maintain peace, Pilate thought it necessary to do with Jesus as they wished. But he also knew that Jesus was innocent. Here, then, was his dilemma—was he to satisfy the demands of the Jews by crucifying Jesus or satisfy the demands of justice by not crucifying Him?

Shrewd fellow that he was, Pilate thought he could extricate himself from the dilemma by appealing to the Jews to feel pity toward Jesus. So he handed Jesus over to a contingent of Roman soldiers to be scourged. The soldiers did as Pilate requested, but they also added a couple of touches of their own by crowning Him with thorns and by clothing Him in a purple robe.

When the process was complete, Pilate brought the bloody and battered Jesus out to the Jewish leaders and exclaimed: "Behold the Man!"

It was Pilate's way of saying: "Look at this poor fellow.

Can't you see that He has suffered enough and that there is no need to go further?"

But these leaders were in no mood for Pilate's scheme. They felt no pity for Jesus at all, but only contempt. And they expressed that contempt by crying: "Crucify Him, crucify Him" (v. 6).

In urging those heartless men to behold Jesus, Pilate wasn't making a theological statement. As far as he was concerned, Jesus was a man and nothing more. Pilate didn't realize that the One beside him was the most extraordinary person who ever lived. Jesus was a man, but He was much more than that. He was also God. He was the God-man.

If Pilate had realized that, he wouldn't have been asking people to pity Jesus. He would have been asking Jesus to pity him, guilty sinner that he was. If he had known the truth about Jesus, he would have fallen on his knees in wondering awe. Because he thought Jesus was an ordinary man, Pilate used the word "behold" to ask those religious leaders to merely look at Jesus. Had he recognized the uniqueness of Jesus, he would have used the word "behold" to call those men to stand in awe before the Lord of Glory. He would have called those men not to merely look at Jesus but rather to see Him. How often we look without seeing when it comes to the truth about Jesus!

Pilate wasn't aware that he was in the arena of the greatest marvel that has ever occurred, the marvel of God taking on our humanity. Do we see the marvel of it, or are we as blind to it as Pilate was?

It was a wonder that the Lord was in our humanity. He didn't have to be. He didn't have to take our humanity at all. He could have stayed in the glory of His heaven. But He took our humanity, and, let's make sure we never miss this: that humanity was real in every respect. It wasn't a pretend humanity.

It's also a wonder what the Lord Jesus did in our humanity. He did something that we haven't done in our humanity. He lived without sin. He refused to break any of God's laws. He never thought an evil thought, never spoke a wrong word, and never did a sinful deed. Having lived that perfect life, He went to the cross to die in our humanity. Death is the penalty for sin. Since Jesus had no sin, He didn't have to die. He died, not for Himself, but for us.

It's also a wonder that Jesus brought our humanity out of the grave, arising from it on the third day just as He promised that He would do.

It's a further wonder that He ascended to heaven in our humanity. He is not in heaven today in exactly the same way that He was before He came. He is there in resurrected, glorified humanity, and that is the guarantee that all who believe in Him will eventually be there with Him in resurrected, glorified humanity.

Pilate was oblivious to the truth of Jesus when he said: "Behold the Man!" He was a politician acting politically. But when I read his words, I say: "Yes, Pilate, let me do exactly that. Let me truly behold the man Jesus."

-14-

From God's Word, the Bible...

"Is it nothing to you, all you who pass by?
Behold and see
If there is any sorrow like my sorrow,
Which has been brought on me,
Which the LORD has inflicted
In the day of His fierce anger.

Lamentations 1:12

Behold His Sorrow

The book of Lamentations, as its title indicates, is a book of grief and mourning. The people of Judah had come under God's judgment, just as the prophets of the Lord had predicted. The Babylonians had invaded their land, destroyed Jerusalem, and carried off a large number of people into captivity. Faith was shaken, families were fragmented, and hopes were dashed.

Jeremiah, one of a small remnant left in the land, bemoans the plight of his people. In this book, he becomes the mouthpiece of the whole nation and reflects their pain and anguish.

In the verse before us, he pictures the nation sitting in desolation beside a road. As people pass by, she calls to them to take note of her condition and to have pity on her.

These words have spurred Christians through the years to think of the Lord Jesus crying these words as He was dying on the cross.

I now try to imagine myself at the foot of His cross. I hear Him asking me to behold His sorrow. And the first thing that comes to my mind is this: *it is a wonder that Christ had any sorrow at all*.

The Lord Jesus didn't begin to exist when He came to this earth. He existed with the Father and the Holy Spirit before the world began. And the triune God was perfectly happy before creation. Each person was happy in Himself, and each was happy with the other.

There wasn't any sorrow in God until sin entered the human race. Even then, God didn't have to feel sorrow. He could have acted in His justice and eternally destroyed Adam and Eve. He could have chosen to be happy with His justice.

Because of His grace, God sorrowed over the sin of His creatures and desired to redeem them. What a marvel it is that God should desire to save us!

Here is the second thing that comes to my mind as I hear the Lord calling me to behold His sorrow: *it is a wonder that Christ could be as sorrowful as He was*.

When He stepped into this world, the Lord Jesus must have found many reasons to rejoice. He must have rejoiced in hearing the birds sing, knowing that He had made them and given them their song. He must have rejoiced in the flowers, knowing that He had given them their delicacy and beauty. He must have rejoiced in the mountains, knowing that He given them their majesty.

But while the Lord Jesus was happy in His world, He became increasingly sorrowful toward the end of His life. When He entered the Garden of Gethsemane, He "began to be sorrowful and deeply distressed." He spoke these words to Peter, James, and John: "My soul is exceedingly sorrowful even to death" (Matt. 26:37-38).

The incredible agony He experienced in Gethsemane was the terrible prelude to a night and day of unspeakable suffering and sorrow. There was the sorrow of His arrest, which denied Jesus passage in the very world that He had created. There was the sorrow of the trials and the mockery. There was the sorrow of being led outside the city as if He was nothing more than garbage to be destroyed.

While these were all causes of indescribable suffering and sorrow, the greatest of all Jesus' sorrows was on the cross itself. There He endured the sorrow of separation from God the Father. The penalty for sin is eternal separation from God. Because Jesus took the place of sinners on the cross to pay the penalty for their sins, He actually had to endure there an eternity of separation from God.

The crux of the cross is this: God put on Christ the very sorrows of hell so all those who believe in Him don't have to experience those sorrows.

Christ would have known no sorrow at all if it hadn't been for us. He took our place. He carried our sorrows (Isa. 53:4-6).

In light of these things, I must also add this: *it is a wonder that we believers don't appreciate more the sorrows that Jesus endured on our behalf.* How often we take His sorrows for granted! How we need to pray:

> *Near the cross! O Lamb of God,*
> *Bring its scenes before me;*
> *Help me walk from day to day,*
> *With its shadows o'er me.*

-15-

From God's Word, the Bible...

"Behold My hands and My feet, that it is I Myself. Handle Me and
see, for a spirit does not have flesh and bones as you see I have."
When He had said this, He showed them His hands and His feet.

Luke 24:39-40

Behold His Hands and Feet

It was the evening of the day Jesus arose from the dead. The eleven disciples of Jesus were in Jerusalem listening to a couple of men who had seen the risen Christ. Suddenly the Lord Himself appeared and said, "Peace to you" (Luke 24:36). We might expect to read that those disciples were overjoyed to see the Lord, but they were terrified because "they supposed they had seen a spirit" (v. 37).

At that point Jesus told them to behold His hands and feet. There was something about those hands and feet to cause those men to wonder and admire. We can look at those same hands and feet through the lens of Scripture and join those disciples in wonder.

The pierced hands and feet of Jesus proved His resurrection. One glance at those hands and feet would have been enough for those disciples to realize that it was their crucified Jesus who was standing before them. One glance? Yes! The wounds created by the nails that held Him on the cross were still visible.

In calling for these men to behold His hands and feet, Jesus was calling for them to behold the truth of His resurrection. And in calling them to behold the truth of His resurrection, He was calling them to be amazed.

The resurrection of Jesus is indeed cause for amazement. Dead people don't just rise from their graves! What does Jesus' resurrection tell us about Him? It tells us that He was not an ordinary man but rather was the person He claimed to be, that is, God in human flesh. It tells us that His death on the cross was satisfying to God the Father. And it tells us that we can trust what Jesus had to say about the reality of sin, the coming of judgment, and the salvation that He came to provide.

The pierced hands and feet of Jesus also proved His resurrection was physical in nature.

This is important. Some people deny that Jesus' body actually came out of the grave. They allege that the disciples felt His presence even though He was dead, and they invented the resurrection stories.

But those pierced hands and feet made it plain that it was Jesus' body that was raised. The body that went into the grave came out of the grave.

Yes, the resurrected body was superior to the body that went into the grave, but it was the same body.

Still further, *the pierced hands and feet of Jesus show what lies ahead of those who die with faith in Christ.* The grave isn't the final destination for our bodies. On the night before He was crucified, Jesus, speaking of His resurrection as if it had already occurred, said to His disciples: "Because I live, you shall live also" (John 14:19).

Believers in Christ are destined to have bodies that are "conformed to His glorious body" (Phil. 3:21).

Finally, *the pierced hands and feet of Jesus reveal the greatness of what He did for His people.*

The Lord took a human body at Bethlehem. He lived and died in that body. He came out of the grave in that body, a vastly superior body to be sure, but still a body. He ascended to the Father in heaven in that body, and He still possesses that body to this very moment.

Here is the extent to which Jesus went to save us—He took our humanity forever. If we were in heaven right now, we could see in the risen body of our Lord Jesus Christ the same pierced hands and feet that His disciples saw when He appeared to them in Jerusalem. Matthew Bridges conveys this truth to us in these wonderful words:

> *Crown Him the Lord of love!*
> *Behold His hands and side,*
> *Those wounds, yet visible above,*
> *In beauty glorified. . . .*

The fact that Jesus is now in heaven in our humanity is the guarantee that all His people will eventually be in heaven with Him in their resurrected, glorified bodies. He is in heaven as our forerunner (Heb. 6:20). He has gone there ahead of us, and His presence there guarantees that we will follow.

As far as I'm concerned, there can be no doubt about it. The most glorious sight in heaven will be the pierced hands and feet of Jesus. What a joy it will be to behold them, realizing as we do that we are in heaven because those hands and feet were pierced on Calvary!

-16-

From God's Word, the Bible...

Behold, He is coming with clouds, and every eye will see Him,
even they who pierced Him. And all the tribes of the earth will
mourn because of Him. Even so, Amen.

Revelation 1:7

.

"Behold, He is Coming"

We've been spending some time with the word "behold." It is a blessed word because it calls us to look so intently that we see the marvel or wonder of the thing that we're seeing.

Some of the things the Bible tells us to behold can't be seen with the eye. We can't see God, but we are to behold Him (Isa. 40:9).

In the verse before us, John urges us to behold something that hasn't yet occurred. He writes of the Lord Jesus: "Behold, He is coming with clouds. . . ."

How do we behold something that is yet to come? We must use the eye of faith. Having faith means we hold with certainty to that which God has revealed to us in His Word. God has revealed that the Lord Jesus will come again. Faith lays hold of that and hangs on to it even though that teaching is often scorned.

The Apostle John was exiled on the Isle of Patmos when

he received from the Lord the revelation that we know as the Book of Revelation (v. 9). This book was addressed to seven of the Lord's churches in Asia Minor. These churches were facing daunting challenges. The need was for them to use the eye of faith to look beyond those challenges to the coming of the Lord.

Our verse consists of thirty-three words, but there are worlds of meaning in those few words. These are some of the most comforting and terrifying words in all of the Bible, and, for that matter, in all of human history. They are comforting to the believer in Christ, and terrifying to the unbeliever. They deal with the revelation of Jesus at the end of human history, just before the Great White Throne Judgment described in Revelation 20.

What does this verse tell us about Christ's coming? First, *it will be a majestic and glorious event.*

The fact that the One who will come is the Lord of Glory (vv. 8,12-18) guarantees that the event itself will be glorious. And the fact that Jesus will come "with clouds" tells us that this will be a grand and magnificent event.

The second thing this verse tells us about the coming of Christ is that *it will be witnessed by all without exception.*

As we noted above, we can't now see with physical eyes the coming of Christ, but that will change when He actually appears. John says: "every eye will see Him."

People throughout history have often been unaware of great events. It is true of people today. But no one will be unaware of this event. "Every eye will see Him."

Does that mean every single eye of every single person who has ever lived? Yes, it most certainly does! What about those who have died? Yes, even those who have died because by this time all of them will have been raised from the dead.

John especially emphasizes that those who "pierced," that is, crucified the Lord Jesus, will see Him. Who does he have in mind? The religious leaders of the Jews? Yes. The Roman soldiers? Yes. Pontius Pilate? Yes.

But in a larger sense, we have all pierced Christ. It was our sins that caused him to be crucified. I was there when He was crucified. I yanked the hammer from the hand of the Roman soldier and drove the nails into Jesus' hands and feet. I joined those soldiers in hoisting the cross into the air. I stood at the foot of the cross with Jesus' haters and added my own words of mockery. Yes, I was there because my sin was there.

The third thing this verse tells us about the coming of Christ is that *it will strike terror into the hearts of "all the tribes of the earth."*

We must take the phrase "all the tribes of the earth" to refer to unbelievers throughout the world. We know it doesn't refer to believers in Christ because John adds: "Even so, Amen." It's obvious that John won't be mourning when Jesus comes. Neither will any believer.

If we don't want to mourn on that day, we must mourn now in repentance and take Christ as our Savior. We must behold Him now as our Savior so we can behold Him without fear when He comes.

-17-

From God's Word, the Bible...

I am He who lives, and was dead, and behold, I am alive forevermore. Amen. And I have the keys of Hades and of Death.

Revelation 1:18

Behold! Alive Forevermore

It was the Lord's Day. The Apostle John was in exile on the Isle of Patmos. The Lord Jesus suddenly appeared to John in dazzling glory (Rev. 1:12-17). John "fell at His feet as dead" (v. 17). Interesting, isn't it? During Jesus' earthly ministry, John had walked with Him as one of His closest disciples, but there is no chummy familiarity here—only awestruck reverence.

Jesus appeared to John to deliver messages of encouragement to seven churches (v. 20). He begins by saying to all of them: "Do not be afraid; I am the First and the Last" (v. 17). He then makes four astounding assertions.

- I am He who lives
- I was dead
- I am alive forevermore
- I have the keys of Hades and of Death

If truth could be likened to real estate, we would have to say that there are vast chunks of ground that Jesus traverses here. In the midst of these assertions, Jesus urges John to "behold." John had beheld so much of Jesus, but he was still called to marvel at what the Lord was saying.

These four assertions can be grouped under two headings. *The first is that the living One died.*

Jesus is the living One. He says: "I am He who lives." This is more than Jesus claiming to be alive at that moment. It is essentially Jesus revealing Himself to be God. God enjoys life that is un-derived and independent. It isn't given to Him or sustained by anyone or anything outside God.

But Jesus also says that He "was dead." How could the Living One die? There was only one way, and that was by taking our humanity. God can't die, but, as we know all too well, humanity can and does.

Jesus took our humanity so that He could die! Why was it necessary? Death is the penalty for our sins—not just physical death, but eternal death. In dying, Jesus took that penalty so all who believe in Him don't have to receive it. Yes, on the cross Jesus received an eternity's worth of God's wrath in the place of sinners.

Our second heading is this: *the dead One is alive forevermore.*

Jesus died, but He didn't stay dead. He arose from the grave, and He lives today to never die again.

Jesus then adds this spectacular statement: "I have the keys of Hades and of Death."

These happy words must be understood in more than one way because death has more than one form.

There is spiritual death. This is the alienation from God that we all have by nature because of our sins. Jesus has the keys to this kind of death. He can and does grant spiritual life to dead sinners. If we were to be locked in a room with no way out, we would be thrilled to hear someone say: "Don't worry, I have the key!" What a happy sound it would be to hear that key turning in the lock! What a delightful sight it would be to see that door swing open! I was once in the gloomy old fortress of spiritual death, but I heard the Lord Jesus say: "Don't worry, I have the key." And the creaky, old door of that fortress swung open. Now I'm free!

Jesus also has the key to physical death. During His earthly ministry, He met a woman on the way to the cemetery to bury her son. But Jesus essentially said to her: "Don't worry. I have the key right here in My pocket." And he raised that young man (Luke 7:11-17).

Jesus used those same keys with Jairus' daughter (Mark 5:22-43), with Lazarus (John 11:38-44), and once again in His own tomb.

The souls of all those who die in faith in Christ go to be with the Lord at the time of their death. But what about their bodies? Does death have the final victory over them? No, Jesus has the keys. When He comes again, He will unlock the graves of all those who know Him. Their bodies will be raised and reunited with their souls. What a day that will be! (1 Thess. 4:13-18).

We who know the Lord know these things, but are we truly beholding them? Are we rejoicing in the glory of them? Do we know anything of stunned wonder as we contemplate them? Our salvation doesn't need to be made more glorious. The need is for us to see the glory that is already there.

-18-

From God's Word, the Bible...

. . . giving thanks to the Father who has qualified us to be partakers of the inheritance of the saints in the light. He has delivered us from the power of darkness and conveyed us into the kingdom of the Son of His love, in whom we have redemption through His blood, the forgiveness of sins.

Colossians 1:12-14

One Fine Stack

Just call the Apostle Paul a "stacker." In this passage, he stacks one phrase on another to give us a magnificent view of salvation through Christ:

- God has qualified us (v. 12);
- God has delivered us (v. 13);
- God has translated us (v. 13);
- God has redeemed us (v. 14);
- God has forgiven us (v. 14).

That's one fine stack! Let's be sure we understand that these things apply only to Christians. Paul was writing to "brethren in Christ" (Col. 1:2) who had "faith in Christ Jesus" (v. 4). And these things all come from God. Salvation is all due to His grace. There is nothing for which any Christian can take credit. The seventeenth-century French theologian Jean Daillé quaintly says of salvation: "This wholly apperteineth unto God."

First, *God has qualified us* to partake of "the inheritance of the saints in the light." That inheritance begins in this life and culminates in heaven. God fits us to share the lot or portion of the saints in this life. This portion is "in the light." Believers, like everyone else, came into this world in a state of spiritual darkness, but God in grace has called them out of that darkness "into His marvellous light" (Eph. 5:8; 1 Peter 2:9). The children of light will finally enter the kingdom of light (Rev. 21:23-25). They will do so only because they have been qualified by the Lord.

We are sinners by nature. We have the darkness of sin in us and with us and, therefore, cannot enjoy the light that God has prepared in eternity. To partake of that, we have to be perfectly righteous. God Himself qualifies sinners to be partakers of the light of glory. In Christ, God provided the righteousness that He demands of us and He applies that righteousness to each believer.

Secondly, *God has delivered us* "from the power of darkness."

We all come into this world as part of Satan's very dark kingdom. The citizens of this kingdom have their minds blinded so they cannot see their true condition (2 Cor. 4:3-4). Those who stay in this kingdom will eventually be enveloped by eternal death (2 Peter 2:17; Jude 12-13).

Believers have been taken out of this kingdom by the Lord Jesus Christ. Through His redeeming death on the cross, He decisively defeated Satan and delivered all believers from his kingdom of darkness.

Thirdly, *God has translated us* "into the kingdom of the Son of His love."

This refers to the practice of removing people from one country and settling them in another. It would have been unspeakably glorious for God to deliver His people from Satan's kingdom, but He also makes them citizens of His own. His kingdom is as light as Satan's is dark.

It is "the kingdom of the Son of His love." How certain believers can be of their new citizenship! God loves His Son with an immeasurable and indestructible love. That same love is extended to all who are in Christ.

Thinking of Christ prompts Paul to add this phrase: "in whom we have redemption through His blood." So *God has redeemed us*.

The word "redeemed" means "bought back." Although believers belonged to God by virtue of creation, they were all taken prisoner by sin and held by the chain of God's law. That law demands that the sinner be punished with eternal separation from God.

But believers have been redeemed by Jesus shedding His blood on the cross. He received there the eternal separation His people deserve. God's law was, therefore, satisfied and they were freed. God paid the ransom for them through the death of His Son.

Finally, Paul tells us that we have in Christ "the forgiveness of sins." In other words, *God has forgiven us*.

To forgive is "to send away" or "to cancel a debt." Satan would have us believe that our sins constitute an insurmountable barrier to entering heaven. He points to those sins and says: "Look at them! You are not fit to enter heaven!"

But we do not fear a creditor pointing to a statement if it has these words stamped on it: Paid in Full. Christians don't fear Satan pointing to their sin debt because Jesus paid it in full.

What a stack this is! It reaches all the way from earth to heaven! How should we respond to it? By "giving thanks to the Father" (v. 12).

-19-

From God's Word, the Bible...

Though He slay me, yet will I trust Him.
Even so, I will defend my own ways before Him.

Job 13:15

Trusting the Lord

Do God's people serve Him only because they enjoy trouble-free lives? Do they stop serving Him when trouble comes?

Many would answer both questions with an emphatic "Yes!" Those who would do so probably haven't heard of Louisa M. Stead.

Louisa, her husband, and their daughter were enjoying a picnic on the coast of Long Island when tragedy occurred. Her husband drowned. There's a good bit of uncertainty about the details. Some accounts say Mr. Stead, in an attempt to save a boy, drowned with the boy. Another account says he saved the boy. Yet another says it was the Steads' daughter, Lily, who was saved by her father. This much we know— Mr. Stead drowned. This occurred in 1879 or 1880.

Trouble had now entered Louisa's life in a major way. How did she respond? Did she stop serving the Lord? She would seem to have had good reason to do so. Instead she and her daughter went to South Africa, where she served as a missionary for fifteen years. After that she married a pastor and served alongside him. The two of them became missionaries in Rhodesia in 1901 and ministered there until their retirement in 1911.

While in South Africa and only two or three years after her first husband's death, Louisa wrote these familiar words:

'Tis so sweet to trust in Jesus, Just to take Him at His Word;
Just to rest upon His promise, Just to know, "Thus saith the Lord!"
Jesus, Jesus, how I trust Him! How I've proved Him o'er and o'er'
Jesus, Jesus, precious Jesus! Oh, for grace to trust Him more!

It's apparent that Louisa had learned the meaning of trusting God. It isn't trusting that God will only do those things that we want done and not do those things that we don't want done. It's rather trusting that God will do what He has revealed in His Word. As we read the Bible, we discover that God has never promised that our lives will be trouble-free. Quite the opposite!

Which of God's many promises did Louisa have in mind when she wrote the first verse of her poem? We find the answer in this verse:

Yes, 'tis sweet to trust in Jesus,
Just from sin and self to cease;
Just from Jesus simply taking
Life and rest, and joy and peace.

The Lord hasn't promised that we will have no trials in life. He has promised to give "life and rest, and joy and peace" if we will trust Him. The "life" must surely mean the abundant life that Jesus promises in John 10:10. The "rest," "joy," and "peace" could refer to several promises, one of which—recorded in Isaiah 26:3—reads:

> *You will keep him in perfect peace,*
> *Whose mind is stayed on You,*
> *Because he trusts in You.*

We see another promise Louisa had in mind here:

I'm so glad I learned to trust Thee, Precious Jesus, Savior, Friend;
And I know that Thou art with me, Wilt be with me to the end.

It's evident that Louisa treasured these words: "For He Himself has said, *'I will never leave you nor forsake you'*" (Heb. 13:5; see also Matt. 28:20).

The Bible offers many marvelous promises. Which one is the greatest? It is God's promise that He will cleanse us from all sin if we will trust in His Son, the Lord Jesus Christ. Louisa M. Stead conveys this in these words:

> *Oh, how sweet to trust in Jesus,*
> *Just to trust His cleansing blood;*
> *And in simple faith to plunge me*
> *'Neath the healing, cleansing flood!*

Much of our success as Christians comes from keeping things in perspective. Do hardships and sorrows come our way in this life? Yes. Do they severely hurt and wound us? Yes. Is it okay to grieve over them? Yes. But our true treasure doesn't lie in the absence of hardship. It rather lies in having our sins forgiven through Christ. Then no trial or difficulty, be it ever so severe, can touch that or change it. So we rejoice in these words from Paul: "For I am persuaded that neither death nor life, nor angels nor principalities nor powers, nor things present nor things to come, nor height nor depth, nor any other created thing, shall be able to separate us from the love of God which is in Christ Jesus our Lord" (Rom. 8:38-39).

-20-

From God's Word, the Bible...

*I marvel that you are turning away so soon from Him who called
you in the grace of Christ, to a different gospel,
which is not another. . .*

Galatians 1:6,7

Three Nots
and One Is (1)

The Apostle Paul usually begins his letters with expressions of appreciation for his readers and with prayer for them but he does not do so in his letter to the Galatians. After wishing his readers grace and peace (v. 3), he plunges right in. There is no time for preliminaries. The issue is far too important for that.

And what is the issue? It is the gospel of Jesus Christ. The Galatians had professed faith in the gospel, but now they were moving away from it.

Paul's love for the gospel wouldn't allow him to take this lightly. So he writes to rebuke them and to call them back to faith in the gospel.

I wonder what Paul would say if he were to write our churches today. Would he accuse us of abandoning the gospel?

On October 31, 1517, Martin Luther stepped to the door of the church in Wittenburg, Germany, and nailed there his nineth-five theses. The sixty-second read: "The treasure of the church is the most holy gospel of the glory and grace of God."

How many churches and pastors today can honestly say the gospel is the treasure of the church? It certainly does not seem so. Pastors load their sermons with tips for living this life, making sure that they add generous doses of humor as they go along. There can't be much talk about sin and judgment because such topics would make their hearers feel bad. If there is no sin and no judgment, there can be no gospel, which is, of course, God's answer to sin and judgment. And if the gospel is not preached, it cannot be called the treasure of the church.

The truth is that we need Paul's words in the above passage as much as the Galatians of old needed them. We can divide those words into four headings, the first of which will receive our attention in today's reading, and the other three in tomorrow's reading. In these four headings, we have the Apostle Paul talking about three things that would seem to be the case, but are not, and one thing that would not seem to be the case but really is.

Paul first mentions *a gospel that is not really a gospel*. He says he is astonished that the Galatians are turning from the gospel of Christ to "a different gospel, which is not another" (v. 6).

The gospel of Jesus Christ is the good news of God's grace. It is the good news of what God has done in and through His Son, the Lord Jesus Christ, to forgive sinners of their sins (v. 4).

But the Galatians were now showing themselves to be soldiers who had deserted the army. They were spiritual deserters! They were now setting aside the gospel of grace to embrace a Christ-plus teaching. John R.W. Stott writes of the Galatians that:

They did not deny that you must believe in Jesus for salvation, but they stressed that you must be circumcised and keep the law as well. In other words, you must let Moses finish what Christ has begun. Or rather, you yourself must finish, by your obedience to the law, what Christ has begun. You must add your works to the work of Christ. You must finish Christ's unfinished work.[3]

Recent surveys indicate that many people today essentially hold the same notion — that salvation is a matter of believing in Jesus and doing good works.

What such people do not understand is that the gospel has to be completely grace or completely works. One negates or cancels out the other. If it is grace, it can't be works. If it is works, it can't be grace (Rom. 4:4; 11:6). Yes, salvation produces good works (Eph. 2:8-10; Titus 2:11-14), but good works do not produce salvation.

If the gospel is a matter of our works, it is not really a gospel at all. The gospel is good news, but there is no good news in salvation by works. It is bad news. God demands perfect righteousness of us, and no matter how many good works we do, we can never do enough.

Let us always be clear on this: we cannot modify or amend the gospel and still have the gospel. After our tampering, we have something, but it is no longer the gospel.

---

[3] John R.W. Stott, *Only One Way: The Message of Galatians*, Inter-Varsity Press, 1968, p. 22.

-21-

From God's Word, the Bible...

. . . but there are some who trouble you and want to pervert the gospel of Christ. But even if we, or an angel from heaven, preach any other gospel to you than what we have preached to you, let him be accursed. As we have said before, so now I say again, if anyone preaches any other gospel to you than what you have received, let him be accursed.

For do I now persuade men, or God? Or do I seek to please men? For if I still pleased men, I would not be a bondservant of Christ.

Galatians 1:7-10

Three Nots
and One Is (2)

In yesterday's reading, we found Paul stressing a gospel that is not really a gospel. Today we look at two additional things that are not true and one thing that is true.

Paul's second emphasis is *teachers who are not really teachers*.

Why had the Galatians gotten into such a mess? It was because of men who "trouble you and want to pervert the gospel" (v. 7), "Judaizers," whose position is stated so clearly by Luke, the author of Acts: "Unless you are circumcised according to the custom of Moses, you cannot be saved" (Acts 15:1).

These men professed to be teachers, but they were actually troublers (the word for "trouble" in verse 7 means to "shake" or "agitate"). Do we understand this? To tamper with the gospel is to trouble the church!

We are living in very difficult and threatening days. Christianity is under attack on every hand. But the greatest danger to Christianity is never the hatred and opposition of those without. It is always those within who pervert the gospel.

Paul's third emphasis is *a choice that should not really be a choice. He* could anticipate some of his readers defending the false teachers: "But, Paul, these men are so brilliant and so interesting. How could they possibly be mistaken?" He answers in the strongest possible way. On one hand, he says, they, the Galatians, have the gospel that "we have preached to you" (v. 8). This is the apostolic message. On the other hand, here comes now "an angel from heaven" (v. 8) to preach another gospel. So they have before them the apostolic message of God's grace and the angelic message of man's works. What should they do? Keep in mind, that the angel is very dazzling and impressive! Many would say that this is a hard choice. But Paul says it should not be a choice at all!

We are not to accept any message on the basis of how impressive the messenger is. We are to judge the messenger by the gospel and not judge the gospel by the messenger!

Having noticed Paul's "nots," we now turn our attention to an "is," namely, *a curse that really is a curse*.

Paul closes this passage by pronouncing a curse, an "anathema" (devoted to destruction) on all those who preach "any other gospel" other than the gospel of the grace of God (v. 9).

Some profess to be upset by Paul's language. They consider it to be an ill-advised, intemperate outburst that is out of keeping with the spirit of Christianity. They think that Paul, if given the opportunity to do so, would take this back or delete these words. But Paul meant every word of this curse, and he meant every word for two reasons: the glory of Christ and the good of men and women.

Paul knew the truth about the person of Jesus. He was not just another man but God in human flesh. Paul also knew why Jesus came to this earth. It was to provide salvation for sinners. If what Jesus did was not sufficient for the salvation of sinners, as the Judaizers insisted, Jesus had failed. And if Jesus failed, there was certainly no point in glorifying His name. So the

Judaizers' teaching robbed Jesus, the God-man, of His glory.

It also robbed people of the hope of salvation. If God in human flesh could not achieve salvation for sinners, what hope was there for those sinners to achieve it for themselves?

With the glory of Christ and the good of sinners in mind, Paul could do no other than pronounce a curse on those who detracted from Christ and the salvation he came to provide. James Denney was right on target when he wrote these words:

> If God has really done something in Christ on which the salvation of the world depends, and if He has made it known, then it is a Christian duty to be intolerant of everything which ignores, denies, or explains it away. The man who perverts it is the worst enemy of God and men.[4]

If we find the Paul's words upsetting, we have all the proof we need that we are not as zealous for the gospel as we should be.

---

[4] James Denney, *The Death of Christ*, Tyndale Publishing House, 1964, p. 66.

-22-

From God's Word, the Bible...

Then He who sat on the throne said, "Behold, I make
all things new." And He said to me,
"Write, for these words are true and faithful."

Revelation 21:5

The Wonder of Ordinary Days

Ordinary days usually have to pass before we appreciate how very wonderful they were. As I was growing up on my family's farm, the days seemed to be, well, so ordinary. Get up, eat breakfast, milk the cows, feed the chickens, go to school, come home, milk the cows—you get the idea.

The people seemed ordinary, too. Dad always wore bib overalls with a faded shirt, and Mom her apron. My brother and I usually wore jeans and shirts that were patched and oftentimes unpatched. I decided when I started my college education in the 1960s that I should get some new clothes. Imagine my surprise when I got there and saw all the students wearing patched and torn clothes! I had been in style for years without realizing it.

Mom's meals were always very good, but also very ordinary. The menu didn't vary much. Even Sunday dinner had an ordinariness about it—consisting always of fried chicken, mashed potatoes, gravy, and a vegetable or two.

Church was ordinary, too. The Sunday School hour was straightforward teaching of the Bible with no bells and whistles. The worship hour always featured the singing of the same old, gnarled hymns. The preaching was always delivered straight from the Bible with no attempts to be chatty and humorous. It was plain and fervent.

Sometimes the ordinariness would make me sigh. It would often seem to be more than I could bear, and I would yearn for something new and exciting. But now I look back on those ordinary days and wish that I could go back and experience again some of what I knew then. I have come to realize over the years that our blessing is in what we have and not in what we don't have. In other words, we can so fret over what we don't have that we fail to appreciate what we do have.

It's good for Christians to look back with nostalgia to the good times of long ago, but our primary look must always be forward. No matter how good the past has been, we Christians can always truthfully say: "The best is yet to come."

What about heaven? Will it be ordinary or extraordinary? The answer, I think, is that it will be both. Heaven ordinary? Yes. When we finally enter our final state—a new earth with a heavenly city (Rev. 21 and 22), lots of things will never change. The streets of gold and gates of pearl will always be in place, as will the twelve foundations. The tree of life will never be barren, and the river of life will never run dry.

But heaven will also be extraordinary. How could it be anything else? We will never get tired of it. The extraordinariness of it will always make the ordinariness of it extraordinary.

And the extraordinariness of heaven won't be just a matter of the beauty of it, but the constant awareness of what we've been saved from. One glance at hell is all we will need to appreciate the glory of heaven. And the extraordinariness of heaven will flow from the constant awareness of how we came to be there, that is, through the redeeming work of Christ. As I've said so often before, the most glorious sight of heaven will be the sight of Christ, and the most glorious sight of Christ will be His nail-pierced hands and feet. Those nail prints will constantly serve as reminders of the tremendous price that He paid on the cross for our redemption.

Heaven will always be the same, but the sameness will never seem same. There will always be greater glories to discover. When we think we have exhausted heaven, we will discover that heaven is inexhaustible.

These well-worn lines catch the blend of both the ordinariness and the extraordinariness of heaven, as expressed by John P. Rees in John Newton's hymn, *Amazing Grace*:

> *When we've been there ten thousand years,*
> *Bright, shining as the sun;*
> *We've no less days to sing God's praise*
> *Than when we first begun.*

Something that can be experienced for ten thousand years must surely have an ordinariness about it. But the fact that all through those years we will be singing God's praise tells us that we will always find heaven to be extraordinary. The challenge before us in ordinary days here is to look beyond them to the ordinary, extraordinary days of heaven.

-23-

From God's Word, the Bible...

Do not marvel that I said to you, "You must be born again."

John 3:7

Brother Lester's Testimony

Brother Lester was a deacon in the first church that I served as pastor. He was a common, ordinary man—just a simple farmer. But he loved the Lord with all of his heart, and he loved to serve the Lord. Brother Lester was one of the most faithful supporters of the church that it has been my privilege to know over the many years of my ministry.

In our evening worship services at Panama Baptist Church, Panama, Illinois, we would occasionally take time for testimonies. Brother Lester would always testify. And he would always begin in exactly the same way, by saying: "I've been a Christian all my life."

Those words must have come as a shock to those who didn't know Brother Lester. We're not born into this world as Christians. But all would become clear when Brother Lester would quickly add his last name. It was Christian. So he was born a Christian—Lester Christian.

Brother Lester would then, in his plain and simple way,

tell us that even though he was born with the name Christian, that didn't really make him a Christian. He had the name from birth, but he didn't really become a Christian until he was saved by the grace of God.

I've heard lots of testimonies over the years, most of which were quite easily forgotten. But I've never forgotten Brother Lester's powerful testimony.

It sounded a warning that many need to hear. I've met some who assumed that they were Christians because they were born and reared in Christian families. I've even met some who assumed that they were Christians because, in their words, "America is a Christian country." I suppose if these people had been born in garages, they would think themselves to be automobiles, or if they had been born in barns, they would think themselves to be cows!

Nicodemus was all tangled up on this issue. It's not enough to merely say he was a Jew. He was eminent among the Jews, having earned for himself the title "the teacher of Israel" (John 3:10).

But with all his learning, Nicodemus didn't understand what is necessary to enable a person to go to heaven. He obviously thought that being born a Jew was synonymous with going to heaven. He equated the two. Jesus pressed home the point that being born physically as a Jew didn't qualify him for heaven. Entering heaven required another kind of birth — a spiritual birth. Jesus put it in these words: "That which is born of the flesh is flesh, and that which born of the Spirit is spirit" (v. 6).

It has become common over the last several years to hear the phrase "born-again Christian." That is repetitive. We might as well say "Christian Christian" for this reason: to be born again is to be a Christian, and to be a Christian is to be born again. There's no entering heaven without being a Christian, and there's no being a Christian without being born again. Jesus said to Nicodemus: "Most assuredly, I say to you, unless one is born again he cannot see the kingdom of God" (v. 3).

This new birth isn't something that we can produce any more than we could produce our physical birth. It is something that takes place as the Spirit of God visits us in regenerating grace. When the Spirit visits us in this way, we come to see how sinful we are and what a dreadful thing it will be to stand before a holy God in our sins. When we come to this point of despair, the Holy Spirit points us to Christ who came from heaven (v. 13) to die on the cross (v. 14) so that we can have salvation from our sins and everlasting life (vv. 15-17). When the Spirit of God enables us to see the enormity of our sins, the horror of coming judgment, and the saving work of Christ, we flee from our sins in repentance and we flee to Christ in faith.

Lester Christian's testimony always served us well. It reminded us that physical birth alone isn't sufficient to enter heaven. We must, by the power of God's Spirit, look to Christ and to Him alone.

-24-

From God's Word, the Bible...

As the deer pants for the water brooks,
So pants my soul for You, O God.
My soul thirsts for God, for the living God.
When shall I come and appear before God?
My tears have been my food day and night,
While they continually say to me,
"Where is your God?"

Psalm 42:1-3

When We Are
Cast Down

Even David didn't live constantly in the warmth of the sunshine of God's presence. Even David knew what it was for the sun to hide behind the clouds and for the cold chill of doubt and uncertainty to creep over him. In this psalm, we find him confessing that his soul was "cast down" (Psalm 42:5,6,11), even to the point that he wept day and night (v. 3). He had gotten so low that he felt completely forsaken by God (v. 9).

How did David get into such a state? Part of it was due to the trouble he was experiencing. He may have written this psalm when his son Absalom tried to replace him as king over Israel. It's clear that David had no access to the Lord's house when he penned this psalm (vv. 2, 4). That was certainly the case when Absalom rebelled against him.

David's trouble was made worse by the taunting of his enemies, who were quick to construe his situation as evidence that he had been wrong to trust in God. If his faith were valid,

God would be helping him! Since God wasn't helping him, his faith was false.

Troubles abound and taunters surround! That's David's sad lament in this psalm.

So what did David do? For one thing, he talked to God. There's a good bit of prayer in this psalm. The fact that God didn't feel near didn't keep David from praying. If we put off praying until God feels near, we won't pray. The trick is to pray until God feels near. We must be careful about making our feelings the engine that pulls the train of prayer. They should be the caboose that follows.

David was very candid in his praying. He didn't try to hide what he was feeling. He honestly admitted this soul was "cast down" (v. 6) and that he felt as if God had forgotten him (v. 9).

One of the great things about God is that He allows us to come to Him to honestly express our doubts, frustrations, and anxieties. God isn't fragile. He won't break.

If we feel that God has forgotten us, let's cry out to Him. Let's seek Him earnestly. It could be that He withdraws from us so He can kindle within us a burning desire for greater evidences of His presence. God's purpose in withdrawing from us may be to make us cry with David:

> *As the deer pants for the water brooks,*
> *So pants my soul for You, O God.*
> *My soul thirsts for God, for the living God.*
> (vv. 1-2a)

If God withdraws from us, we may rest assured that it is so He may come back to us in a larger way.

Yes, David talked to God in the midst of his troubles and his taunters. But he also talked to himself. He reproved or reproached himself. Twice he says:

Why are you cast down, O my soul?
And why are you disquieted within me?
(vv. 5, 11)

Having reproved himself, David begins to reason with himself. He recalls evidences of God's faithfulness in the past (v. 6) and he assures himself that God will be lovingly kind to him in the present (v 8).

Reproving himself and reasoning with himself! That's what David did. In doing so, he shows us the art of dealing with ourselves. He urges us when we are in trouble to stop listening to ourselves and to start talking to ourselves. That sounds like nonsense, but it is really a vital principle. We are listening to ourselves when we allow ourselves to think of all the things that are against us, saying: "Just look. I have all these troubles and all these people who are opposed to me. Why can't it be the way it was a few years ago?" And on and on we go.

We stop listening to ourselves when we begin to call to mind what we know about God. Although He seems to withdraw from us, He will never completely abandon or forsake us. Although our problems may seem to indicate otherwise, He loves us with an undying love. Although our problems can be great, our God is always greater. How do we know these things? They are all in the Bible, the book of God's love. That same book also tells us about the greatest evidence of God's love for us—the unspeakably wonderful gift of His Son who provided a full salvation to all who would call upon Him.

-25-

From God's Word, the Bible...

"Lord, now You are letting Your servant depart in peace,
According to Your word;
For my eyes have seen Your salvation."

Luke 2:29-30

What Simeon Says

We're familiar with the children's game *Simon Says*. The game starts with someone being designated as Simon. The role of Simon is to give commands to the other children. Every command that begins with "Simon says" must be obeyed. But if any obey a command that doesn't begin with those words, they are out of the game. The game continues until everyone is out except one. That person wins and becomes the next Simon.

To win the game, players must listen very carefully to "Simon." In Luke 2:25-35, we meet, not a Simon, but a Simeon. He has such important things to say to us that we must carefully listen.

He is speaking now from the pages of Scripture. Can you hear him? He first speaks to us *about fulfillment*.

Mary and Joseph had brought the baby Jesus to the temple "to present Him to the Lord" (v. 22). Simeon was there. He is described to us as "just and devout" (v. 25). He was also a waiting man. He was waiting "for the Consolation of Israel" (v. 25). That means that he was waiting for the Messiah to come.

God first promised the coming of the Messiah to Adam and Eve in Genesis 3:15. That was many centuries before Simeon ever made his appearance on the human stage. Many may have begun to doubt whether the Messiah would ever come. Not Simeon! And when he saw Mary and Joseph there at the temple with Jesus, he realized that the one for whom he had been waiting had arrived. A flash of revelation from God let Simeon know that Jesus was the Messiah. So Simeon took Jesus "up in his arms and blessed God" (v. 28).

Imagine holding your eternal salvation in your own arms and looking at it with your own eyes! That's what Simeon did. It's even better to hold that salvation in our hearts, and that we can all do by trusting in Christ as our Savior.

Let's listen to Simeon again. Now he is speaking to us *about being Spirit-filled*. Luke mentions the Holy Spirit three times in verses 26 and 27. The Holy Spirit was "upon" Simeon (v. 25). The Holy Spirit had revealed truth to Simeon (v. 26). The Holy Spirit had led Simeon to the temple (v. 27). I would summarize all of that by saying Simeon was Spirit-filled.

What is it to be filled with the Spirit? It's not a matter of being highly emotional, as some imagine. It's rather a matter of being focused on the Lord Jesus. The more Christ-centered we are, the more Spirit-filled we are. We must always remember that the Holy Spirit's primary task is to exalt Christ (John 16:14).

Let's listen to Simeon yet again. Now he is speaking to us *about a matter of immense importance—dying*.

Simeon had received a promise from the Lord that he wouldn't die until he had seen the Messiah (v. 25). That promise was now fulfilled as he held Jesus in his arms. Having seen Jesus, Simeon was ready to die. He says:

> *Lord, now you are letting*
> *Your servant depart in peace,*

According to Your word. . .
(v. 29)

If we were reading Simeon's words in Latin, we would find the first two words to be "nunc" (now) "dimittis" (dismiss). "Now dismiss," is what he says to the Lord.

We're all facing dismissal from this life. We all have an appointment with death (Heb. 9:27). Death is not only coming most surely upon us but also most rapidly upon us. A few years ago, I went to visit a man in the hospital. He held his forefinger about a half-inch away from his thumb and said: "Life lasts about that long."

Yes, life speeds by, and then our dismissal comes.

But we can face our dismissal with peace. J.C. Ryle writes of Simeon:

> He speaks like one for whom the grave has lost its terrors, and the world its charms. He desires to be released from the miseries of this pilgrim-state of existence, and to be allowed to go home. . . .He speaks as one who knows where he is going when he departs this life, and cares not how soon he goes.[5]

What gave Simeon peace in the face of dismissal? His faith in the Lord Jesus! If we are to enjoy Simeon's peace, we must share his faith.

.

---

[5] J.C. Ryle, *Expository Thoughts on Luke*, The Banner of Truth Trust, 1986, Vol. i, p. 67

-26-

From God's Word, the Bible...

"But of that day and hour no one knows, not even the angels of heaven, but My Father only."

Matthew 24:36

The Devil
in the Dates

It has happened again. This time it was "a Christian numerologist" who set the date for Christ's return. The date was April 23, 2018. I'm writing this chapter on April 26, 2018. What does that tell you? It tells you that once again a prediction of the Lord's return didn't come true.

I say "once again" because this has happened several times over the years. One such prediction that the Lord would come on May 21, 2011, was widely reported in the news.

I have never been able to understand why so-called "Christian leaders" feel the need to set a date for Christ's coming when the Lord Jesus Himself so plainly said no one will know the day or the hour when it will occur. The thing we most need to know about the date of His coming is that we don't know it. And we can't know it. Preachers don't know it. Scholars don't know it. Even the angels of heaven don't know it. Only God the Father knows when the Lord Jesus will come again, and I think if someone should guess the date by accident, the Lord would change it.

So someone set a date for the Lord's return, and it didn't happen. Does it really matter? Why make a big deal out of it? It does matter, and it is a big deal. The problem, you see, is the devil gets into this date-setting business. He uses the failures of the date setters to discredit Christianity. He claps his hands in glee when we make Christianity look foolish in the eyes of the world.

On the matter of the Lord's return, the Bible doesn't put the emphasis on the time of it. To the contrary, the Lord Jesus said to His disciples: "It not for you to know times or seasons which the Father has put in His own authority" (Acts 1:7).

Here's where the Bible puts the emphasis: "Therefore, since all these things will be dissolved, what manner of persons ought you to be in holy conduct and godliness. . .?" (2 Peter 3:11).

The Lord's coming is not a date to be circled on the calendar. It's a trumpet call to godliness!

It should be enough for us to know that the Lord is coming. The Bible testifies to the certainty of this with very emphatic statements from Jesus (John 14:3), the angels (Acts 1:11), the Apostle Paul (1 Thess. 4:16), the author of Hebrews (Heb. 10:37), and the Apostle John (1 John 3:2).

When He comes, He will bring with Him the souls of all those believers who have died, will raise their bodies from their graves, and will reunite those souls and bodies. He will also catch up or snatch away those believers who are still living on the earth. Without having to pass through death, these people will see their limited, frail, mortal bodies transformed into bodies such as the Lord Jesus now has (Phil. 3:20-21). All of this will happen in the blink of an eye (1 Cor. 15:51-52).

With such glorious things of which we can be certain, why should we focus our attention on something that is uncertain, that is, the date at which it will all occur?

It's okay for Christians to appear foolish in the eyes of the world if our foolishness is where God wants it to be. The cross of Christ is the point at which God wants us to appear foolish. Paul writes: "For the message of the cross is foolishness to those who are perishing, but to us who are being saved it is the power of God" (1 Cor. 1:18).

A man dying on a cross to provide salvation for sinners? It seems so utterly absurd. But that cross brings glory to God, and in His own time, He will show it to be the greatest wisdom. God uses that cross to humble sinners so He can bring them to Himself in repentance and faith.

Setting the date for the Lord's coming is different. It brings no glory to God because He has told us to not do it. It's rather an attempt of men to bring glory to themselves. The devil always applauds every one of our sad attempts to exalt ourselves.

-27-

From God's Word, the Bible...

*Moreover the L*ORD *said to me, "Take a large scroll, and write on it with a man's pen concerning Maher-Shalal-Hash-Baz. And I will take for Myself faithful witnesses to record, Uriah the priest and Zechariah the son of Jeberechiah."*

*Then I went to the prophetess, and she conceived and bore a son. Then the L*ORD *said to me, "Call his name Maher-Shalal-Hash-Baz; for before the child shall have knowledge to cry 'My father' and 'My mother,' the riches of Damascus and the spoil of Samaria will be taken away before the king of Assyria."*

Isaiah 8:1-4
(Read the whole passage in Isaiah 8:1-8.)

God at Work in His World

Isaiah chapter 8 is part of what is sometimes called "The Book of Immanuel." This section, reaching from Isaiah 7:1 to 12:6, is rich with promises about the coming Messiah (e.g., 7:14; 9:6-7; 11:1-5,10).

This portion of Isaiah was written at a particularly tense time. Armies were marching, kings were plotting, and people were grumbling. All were trembling.

We can't understand these times if we fail to distinguish between four kingdoms: Judah, Israel, Syria, and Assyria.

Assyria, the power of the day, was gobbling up smaller nations. The kings of Judah, Israel, and Syria were very alarmed. What were they to do?

The obvious way for a weak country to make itself stronger is by forming an alliance with another nation. Israel and Syria did this, and they were pressuring Judah to join them.

But Ahaz, king of Judah, had what he considered to be a

better idea. He decided to form an alliance with Assyria, that gobbler of other nations.

No sooner had Ahaz done this than he realized he now had another problem. The kings of Israel and Syria were so enraged by his alliance with Assyria that they decided to invade Judah.

In trying to save himself from one enemy (Assyria), Ahaz had created for himself a new enemy (the allied Israel and Syria), and this new enemy was much closer to home.

Ahaz was so scared that ". . . his heart and the heart of his people were moved as the trees of the woods are moved with the wind" (Isa. 7:2).

Into this troubled situation, God sent Isaiah to deliver a message to Ahaz. It was a message about quick and easy pickings (vv. 1-4), surging waters (vv. 5-8), and Immanuel (v. 8).

The quick and easy pickings part amounted to God assuring Ahaz that he didn't need to worry about Israel and Syria because God was going to make those nations quick and easy pickings for Assyria.

God conveyed this message to Isaiah by announcing that he and his wife were to have a son whom they were to name Maher-Shalal–Hash-Baz, which means "quick and easy pickings." Before this baby could say "Momma" or "Dada," Israel and Syria would be destroyed by Assyria.

The *surging waters part* of the prophecy dealt with the future of Judah. The fact that Israel and Syria would be destroyed didn't mean that Judah was home free. God was displeased with the alliance Ahaz had made with Assyria. He had made it clear that the nation of Judah was to depend on Him for its security—not on alliances with godless nations.

The Lord chose to picture this in terms of rivers. He says the people of Judah had essentially refused the softly flowing water of one river to launch out on the extremely turbulent and treacherous water of another.

The softly flowing river was God's government. The turbulent and treacherous river was Assyria with whom the people of Judah were now allied. They, the people of Judah, would find that the waters they had chosen would be too much for them, coming up to their necks and threatening to completely overflow them! We can see the fulfillment of this prophecy by reading 2 Kings 18 and 19.

The Immanuel part of the prophecy amounts to God allowing Ahaz to listen to what God the Father had to say to His Son, the Messiah, who would be called Immanuel (God with us). In verse 8, God assures the Messiah that the land of Judah wouldn't be destroyed, and that there would still be a land into which He would come.

Nations, kings, alliances from centuries ago! It's enough to make the head swim! Can these things have any meaning for us? They do indeed! They remind us that God isn't shut out of His world. He knows every detail, and He is involved in all the events. These things also remind us that God is often at work in this world in judgment. Many of the things we interpret as results of political decisions are really evidences of God judging human disobedience. These things also show us that nothing that is going on in the world will keep God from fulfilling His promises. The turbulence of that era didn't keep Christ from coming, and the turbulence of our era won't keep Him from coming again. So let's trust God in the turbulence.

In all these things, whether in times of turmoil or times of relative peace, the ageless gospel of God's reconciling work through His Messiah—Jesus—is offered to sinners. Even if you live in troubled times, you may still know peace with God through our Lord Jesus Christ, God's Immanuel.

-28-

From God's Word, the Bible...

*Then news of these things came to the ears of the church in
Jerusalem, and they sent out Barnabas to go as far as Antioch.
When he came and had seen the grace of God, he was glad, and
encouraged them all that with purpose of heart they should
continue with the Lord. For he was a good man, full of the Holy
Spirit and of faith. And a great many people
were added to the Lord.*

Acts 11:22-24

Mr. Encourager

Barnabas didn't start out as Barnabas. His name when he became a Christian was Joses. There was nothing wrong with that name. It meant "increaser." His parents may have given it to him to express their hope that he would become a prosperous man.

But while Joses was a good name, it just didn't seem to fit. As the early disciples spent time with Barnabas, they felt strange calling him "increaser." They couldn't be around him very long without him encouraging them in some way. It didn't matter what their circumstances were, Barnabas encouraged them. If they lost a loved one, he encouraged them. If they became weary in the Lord's work, he encouraged them. If they felt inadequate for their tasks, he encouraged them. If they felt guilty over a sin, he encouraged them. If they were fearful of what the future might bring, he encouraged them.

Because Barnabas unfailingly encouraged all those around him, it became as natural as breathing for his fellow-Christians to call him "encourager." That's what the name Barnabas means (Acts 4:36).

One example of Barnabas' encouraging ministry is seen in the case of the Apostle Paul. After he was converted to Christ on the road to Damascus, Paul, then known as Saul of Tarsus, found difficulty in aligning himself with the disciples of the Lord Jesus. They were all afraid of this man who had been the most vigorous and unrelenting persecutor of the church. Perhaps his "conversion" was nothing more than a clever ruse to carry out further persecution!

Barnabas stepped into that situation. He brought Saul before the disciples and explained to them how he had found the Lord, or, we should say how the Lord found him (Acts 9:26-27). In doing so, Barnabas broke down he barrier between Saul and the other Christians and brought peace. That is the type of thing an encourager does!

When we encounter Barnabas again, this time at Antioch, we find him still encouraging. Seeing many new converts, Barnabas took a personal interest in them and encouraged them to remain true to the Lord (Acts 11:23).

Barnabas, it seems, never missed an opportunity to do whatever was necessary. He spoke encouraging words, and he did encouraging things.

We need the example of Barnabas. These are very discouraging days, and God's people seem to be a very discouraged lot. Sometimes the discouragement comes to us because of the times in which we live—times of increasing hostility toward Christians. We're seeing more and more of this hostility expressed in outright persecution. Sometimes the discouragement is personal in nature. We have committed a grievous sin or we have labored hard for the Lord without success. Or it may be that we are facing a very taxing problem such as sickness, conflict with someone, or the loss of a loved one.

There are many reasons for discouragement, and there are many discouraged Christians. It is vital, therefore, for us to become encouragers as Barnabas was.

We certainly can't leave Barnabas without asking how he came to be the way that he was. What made him such an encourager? We must attribute it to the grace of God that worked in him. Barnabas was saved by grace and equipped by grace. But we must go further. The grace of God worked in all those early saints, but Barnabas stood out among them.

Perhaps the clue to Barnabas is found in these words: ". . . he was a good man, full of the Holy Spirit and of faith" (Acts 11:24).

Barnabas was a full man! Full of the Holy Spirit! Full of faith! Our days cry for Christians to be full men and women—not filled with money, career, pleasure, and sports—but filled, as Barnabas was, with the Holy Spirit and faith. If we would be like Barnabas, we must be filled with those things that filled him.

How do we become filled with the Holy Spirit and with faith? There is only one way, and that is by being filled with the Word of God. Do we want more of the Spirit? The Word of God is "the sword of the Spirit" (Eph. 6:17). Do we want more of faith? Faith comes by hearing, and hearing by the Word of God (Rom. 10:17).

Barnabas will never make the list of the best-known men in the Bible. But he certainly deserves our admiration and emulation.

-29-

From God's Word, the Bible...

Who is this coming up from the wilderness,
Leaning upon her beloved?
I awakened you under the apple tree.
There your mother brought you forth;
There she who bore you brought you forth.

Song of Solomon 8:5

Coming up from the Wilderness

The Song of Solomon is the love song of the Bible. It relates in poetic form how King Solomon of Israel fell in love with a country girl, a Shulamite, and took her to be his wife.

In this verse, the happy couple is seen walking back toward the city after taking a stroll through a barren, wilderness area. Someone, perhaps a relative of the Shulamite, sees them approaching and exclaims:

> *Who is this coming up from the wilderness,*
> *Leaning upon her beloved?*

These aren't the words of one who was ignorant of the bride's identity, but rather the words of one who is happily taking note of what has taken place. The Shulamite girl is now the wife of the king! Who would have ever thought such a thing could happen? Here, then, is what this person was saying: "Can this be the simple country girl that I know who is now walking with the king?"

The one who uttered these words was filled with wonder over what he was seeing.

The Song of Solomon pictures for us a love that is even more wonderful—that which Christ has for His church and which His church has for Him.

Now here is something to marvel about: the church of Christ is coming up out of the wilderness, leaning all the while on her Beloved!

This world is very much like a wilderness for God's people—filled with difficulties and taxing our resources. Why is it this way? The Bible gives us the answer. This world didn't start out this way. The world has gone from being a garden to a wilderness, and sin is the reason. Sin is the great wrecker. It never improves or upgrades anything. It only ruins.

While Christians often sigh as they walk through this wilderness, they have a reason to rejoice. The church of which they are a part is coming out of the wilderness. The reason the church is on her way out of the wilderness is that she has a Beloved. She has One who loves her more than words can express, and One whom she loves.

The church's Beloved is the Lord Jesus Christ. He is the One who set His love on the church even before time began. He saw her there in the wilderness of the world, and, because of His love for her, He Himself decided to go into the wilderness to bring her out. This brought Him all the way from heaven to the cross where He endured the wrath of God in the place of His church.

Someday the church's walk through this wilderness will be over. The Lord Jesus who now walks with her through His Spirit will lead her out. What a glorious day that will be! He will escort her to join Him in heaven. Heaven won't be a wilderness. Wilderness living will be forever gone when Jesus comes for His people.

So we wait for that splendid day, but we wait in the wilderness. How do we go about this business of waiting? How do we handle the hardships, disappointments, and sorrows of wilderness living while we wait? Our text gives us the answer. We must lean on our Beloved One, the Lord Jesus.

That word "leaning" is rich in implications. It means that the church is conscious of her own weakness. She realizes that the wilderness is too much for her if she is left to her own strength.

But it also means that the church is keenly aware that her Beloved does have the resources that wilderness living demands. Isn't it encouraging to know that the Lord cares enough for us to allow us to lean on Him? He sympathizes with us (Heb. 4:15-16), and He urges us to trust Him. So let us lean on Christ.

As we lean on him, let's trust Him in every circumstance of life. Let's trust Him to care. Let's trust Him to strengthen us. Let's trust Him to have a purpose for us in the midst of our difficulties. Let's trust Him to finally bring us out of the wilderness. Let's trust every promise He has given in His Word. Let's lean on our Beloved, singing as go:

Leaning, leaning,
Safe and secure from all alarms;
Leaning, leaning,
Leaning on the everlasting arms.
(Elisha A. Hoffman)

-30-

From God's Word, the Bible...

Yes, and all who desire to live godly in Christ Jesus will suffer persecution.

2 Timothy 3:12

The Happiness
in the Hatred

I hate to be hated. I want to be liked. But I am hated, increasingly so, it seems, by people who don't even know me. The reason is that I'm a Christian.

Hostility toward Christians is growing by leaps and bounds all around the world, even in countries founded on Judeo-Christian principles. Large numbers of people seem to be oblivious to this problem. That's not surprising. Many in the news media find it convenient to ignore it because they harbor hostility toward Christians themselves.

How are we to explain this hatred? Christians just seem to be so out of step! They insist on believing that God created the world, that humans are fundamentally flawed by sin, and are in need of forgiveness. They continue to insist that there's a judgment to come, and, very annoyingly, they maintain that there's only one way for people's sins to be forgiven and that way is Christ. Such beliefs fly in the face of the accepted dogmas of the day.

And there's an increasing tendency these days to link Christianity with all that has been wrong with the world in the past. As far as many are concerned, Christianity is the religion of white people who enjoy oppressing people with other skin colors! Have Christians failed in many ways through the centuries? Yes. But Christians have also been in the forefront of correcting many of the ills of society. By the way, not all are Christians who claim to be such. It's good to keep that in mind when attributing failures to "Christians" down through the centuries.

At the root of much of the hatred toward Christianity is the belief that it is an impediment to creating the kind of world that the haters want and, therefore, it must be destroyed.

One example of hatred for Christians surfaced on Facebook when a photo was posted of Christian teenagers at a restaurant giving thanks for their food. The reaction was swift, and, in many cases, severe. One person wrote: "I'm so tired of the arrogance many religious people display and their disdain for non-believers." Another person responded: "So tired of Christians pushing their beliefs onto everyone else."

Simply giving thanks for a meal is showing "disdain" for unbelievers? Who knew? It's a way of "pushing" their beliefs on others? If these Christian teenagers had stood up in the restaurant and said: "We are going to pray over our food, and we want you all to be quiet," that would constitute "pushing their beliefs" on others. But that's not what happened. And why is it that the critics of Christianity don't apply the same standard to themselves? Do they worry about pushing their beliefs on to others? Ask Christian bakers and florists about that!

Yet another response read: "If you are confidant (*sic*), in your beliefs then you don't feel the need to 'save' everyone else."

That's hilarious! Nothing is more common these days than those on the left of the political spectrum trying to "save" the rest of us from bias, climate change, economic injustice, guns, knives, sodas, micro-aggressions, and sexual hang-ups. It's not that those on the left are wrong on every issue. It's rather that they tend to think no one is entitled to an opinion except themselves.

While I don't enjoy being hated for my beliefs, I have to say that I find some happiness in the hatred. One reason is that it confirms the teaching of the Lord Jesus, who said: "If you were of the world, the world would love its own. Yet because you are not of the world, but I chose you out of the world, therefore the world hates you" (John 15:19).

Another part of my happiness in the midst of the world's hatred comes from knowing that the Lord will be with His people to strengthen and help them. The Apostle Paul, who knew very well what it was to be hated for Christ, was able to say in the midst of it: "But the Lord stood with me and strengthened me. . ." (2 Tim. 4:17a).

There's also happiness in knowing that the faith I hold dear will eventually prove to be triumphant. The Apostle John says: "And this is the victory that has overcome the world—our faith" (1 John 5:4b).

While the Christian-haters can destroy Christian buildings, businesses, and bodies, they can't destroy Christianity. The only way for that to occur is for the Christ on whom it is built to be destroyed. That can't happen.

-31-

From God's Word, the Bible...

You number my wanderings;
Put my tears into Your bottle;
Are they not in Your book?

Psalm 56:8

The Bottle

Psalm 56 is a prayer. The New King James Version supplies this heading for the psalm: *Prayer for Relief from Tormentors*. Under that title is the note that David wrote it when he was captured by the Philistines in Gath (1 Sam. 21:10-15).

I've never had much trouble with the first seven verses. David cries to God for mercy because he feels that his enemies are about to "swallow" him. No problem understanding that. He says his enemies "hound" him "all day." Yep, got that. He says he will trust in God when he is afraid. Copy that.

But I always found verse 8 to be a bit befuddling, especially that "bottle" business. I took David's phrase about God "numbering" his "wanderings" or "flutterings" to mean that he would not have one more difficulty than the number God had allotted to him. It's comforting to know that our trials, no matter how numerous, have an end. For believers in Christ, they don't last forever.

And I took David's phrase about his flutterings already being in God's "book" to mean that there is a purpose behind all of them. That purpose is recorded in God's book of explanation, the book which will be read to God's people when they get home to heaven. All of our trials will then make perfect sense.

But what about that bottle? What did David mean when he asked God to put his tears into His bottle? Some suggest that he was asking God to always remember his trials, as if God could forget.

It finally occurred to me that for someone to catch our tears in a bottle that person would have to be very near to us. No one can catch tears in a bottle if he or she is standing ten or twenty feet away.

So I think David was asking God to be very near him as he was facing trouble. Nothing helps us more when we are in horrible circumstances than knowing that our God is near, near to sympathize, to strengthen, to encourage, to uphold. When problems mount up around us, we not only want God to be near; we want Him to make us know that He is near.

In August of 1932, Thomas A. Dorsey was leading the singing in a church service in St. Louis, Missouri. Someone handed him a telegram that contained these brutal words: "Your wife just died." He called home, but the person who answered could only frantically repeat these words: "Nettie is dead! Nettie is dead!"

Dorsey immediately enlisted a friend to drive him home. When he arrived, he received another jolt of devastating news. His baby boy had also died.

After going through the first few days of horrible grief, Dorsey said: "I began to feel that God had done me an injustice. I didn't want to serve Him anymore or write any more gospel songs."

But something happened a few days later to change his mind. Feeling a calmness coming over his spirit, he went to the piano and began to play. Here's how he described it: "As my fingers began to manipulate over the keys, words began to fall in place on the melody like drops of water falling from the crevice of the rock." Those words are well known among Christians:

> *Precious Lord, take my hand,*
> *Lead me on, help me stand;*
> *I am tired, I am weak, I am worn*
> *Thru the storm, thru the night,*
> *Lead me on to the light,*
> *Take my hand, precious Lord,*
> *Lead me home.*
>
> *When my way grows drear,*
> *Precious Lord, linger near;*
> *When my life is almost gone,*
> *Hear my cry, hear my call,*
> *Hold my hand, lest I fall;*
> *Take my hand, precious Lord,*
> *Lead me home.*

The Lord has to be very near us to take us by the hand or to catch our tears in a bottle.

"I wish," someone says, "that I could be sure that the Lord is near enough to take me by the hand or to catch my tears."

Look to Jesus. His name is Immanuel, which means "God with us." Because Jesus took our humanity, it's true to say that He sympathizes with us in our humanity, but, true as that is, it's not quite strong enough. It's rather that because Jesus took our humanity, He can't help but sympathize with us. And, sympathizing with us, He holds our hands and His bottle.

That same Jesus also experienced tears. He is a sympathetic high priest to all who come to God through Him and He promises mercy and grace to help in time of need (Heb. 4:14-16); have you come to Him? Are you on your way to heaven?

About the Author

Roger Ellsworth is a retired pastor, active in ministry and writing, who lives in Jackson, Tennessee. He and his wife, Sylvia, love the message of the Bible, and they enjoy sharing the wonderful counsel of the Word of God in language that ordinary people can understand and appreciate.

Roger has written numerous books on the Christian faith, and has exercised a preaching ministry for over fifty years. His sermons are available to listen for free on SermonAudio.com.

The Series

Enjoy collecting the My Coffee Cup Meditations Series.

A Dog and A Clock 978-0-9988812-9-4 (Series#1)
The "Thumbs-Up" Man 978-0-9988812-5-6 (Series#2)
When God Blocks Our Path 978-0-9988812-4-9 (Series#3)
Fading Lines, Unfading Hope 978-0-9996559-1-7 (Series#4)
The Day the Milk Spilled 978-0-9965168-6-0 (Series#5)
"Where Are the Donuts?" 978-0-9965168-7-7 (Series#6)
Sure Signs of Heavenly Hope 978-0-9988812-1-8 (Series#7)
My Dog Knows It's Sunday 978-0-9996559-6-2 (Series#8)
Rover and the Cows 978-0-9996559-7-9 (Series#9)
Apples of Gold in Settings of Silver (Series#10)
Old Houses, New Houses (Series#11)
The Golden Key on the Silver Chain (Series#12)

Collect All the Books!

www.mycoffeecupmeditations.com